Evangelism for the 21st Century

Dr. Kevin Riggs

EVANGELICAL TRAINING ASSOCIATION
PO Box 327, Wheaton, IL 60187

Evangelism for the 21st Century

Copyright © 2014 Evangelical Training Association. All rights reserved. No part of this book may be reproduced without written permission, except for brief quotations in books, critical articles, and reviews. Appropriate citations required.

Scripture quotations are taken from The HOLY BIBLE, NEW INTERNATIONAL VERSION®. Copyright © 1973, 1978, 1984 by International Bible Society. Used by permission of Zondervan Publishing House. All rights reserved. The "NIV" and "New International Version" trademarks are registered in the United States Patent and Trademark Office by International Bible Society. Use of either trademark requires the permission of International Bible Society.

Scripture marked (KJV) is from the King James Version.

Scripture marked (NKJV) is taken from the *New King James Version*. Copyright © 1979, 1980, 1982 by Thomas Nelson, Inc. Used by permission. All rights reserved.

Scripture marked "New American Standard Bible" is taken from the NEW AMERICAN STANDARD BIBLE ®, Copyright © 1960, 1962, 1963, 1968, 1971, 1972, 1973, 1975, 1977, 1995 by The Lockman Foundation. Used by permission.

Scripture marked (NABRE) is taken from The New American Bible, revised edition © 2010, 1991, 1986, 1970 Confraternity of Christian Doctrine, Inc., Washington, DC. All Rights Reserved.

ISBN: 978-1-929852-88-8

Printed in the United States of America

Table of Contents

Introduction 5

1 A Biblical Definition of Evangelism 7

2 Evangelism and the Kingdom of God 17

3 Evangelism in the Early Church 27

4 Evangelism and the Local Church 37

5 Evangelism as a Spiritual Gift 47

6 Evangelism and Personal Responsibility 57

7 Evangelism and the Whole Person 67

8 Evangelism and Social Justice (Part 1) 77

9 Evangelism and Social Justice (Part 2) 89

10 Evangelism in a Post-Christian World 99

11 Evangelism and the Family 109

12 Evangelism and the Great Commission 119

Introduction

It's 5:15 a.m. on a Sunday morning—time to roll out of bed and get ready for a full day of local church ministry. As I wipe the sleep from my eyes, I notice I have a new email on my smartphone. The email is from a former student, a Muslim from Iraq who wants to talk to me about Christianity. *Wow!* I think to myself, *An open door for evangelism.*

However, as I continue reading the email, I quickly realize my former student does not really want to talk to me about Christianity. He wants to convert me to Islam! He is trying to "evangelize" me!

Over the next few weeks we correspond back and forth, but to no avail. I am still a Christian. He is still a Muslim. I think we are still friends.

What would it take to evangelize a person from another faith?

Several years ago, I moved back to my hometown to restart a church that had died. For the first eight months, we met on Sunday evenings. For eight months, I had Sunday mornings free. Sometimes on Sunday mornings, I would drive to the local coffee shop. I live in the "Bible Belt." It surprised me as I drove around how many people in my community did not attend church. Many times during those drives for coffee, I asked myself, "What would it take to reach these people for Christ?"

In addition to pastoring, I teach sociology at a local community college. Many of my students are unchurched and uninterested in anything related to Christianity. I look at my students and I look at the average church in my city, and I see a disconnect. I know that sounds harsh, but that is what I observe. I wonder, "What would have to happen for my students to become interested enough to walk through those church doors?"

I don't have the answer. If you are looking for a "how-to" book, this is not it. This book is about the principles of living out your faith in your world with the conviction that as you live out your faith, people will notice and ask questions. The premise of this book is Peter's admonishing, "But in your hearts set apart

Christ as Lord. Always be prepared to give an answer to everyone who asks you to give the reason for the hope that you have" (1 Peter 3:15).

Another premise of this book is that evangelism is primarily about God's kingdom breaking into present reality through faith in Jesus Christ. Evangelism is more than a memorized prayer. It is more than simply getting people to attend church. Evangelism encompasses every area of life, from personal salvation to social justice to environmental concerns. In and through Jesus, all life is changed. Faith in Jesus makes us citizens of God's kingdom, and that citizenship is a present reality as well as a future hope.

A third premise is that evangelism is the 21st century looks a lot like evangelism in the first century. And that is a good thing! The believers in the first century turned their world upside down. We have the tremendous opportunity to do the same thing.

1
A Biblical Definition of Evangelism

As I knock on the door, I simultaneously hope no one is home and someone is home.

I am used to the routine. Every Thursday afternoon (weather permitting), some fellow high school classmates from our Christian school and I canvas the neighborhood doing "door-to-door visitation."

A single mom with a toddler on her hip answers the door. She is out of breath, her hair is disheveled, and her eyes communicate she has not seen peace and quiet in a long time.

I begin the routine: "Good afternoon. My name is Kevin and this is my friend, Mike, and we are from Evangelical Christian Academy. Do you mind if I ask you a question?"

The obviously haggard mom politely says she doesn't mind. Undaunted, I ask, "If you died right now do you know if you would go to heaven or hell?"

There is no, "How are you doing?" "What's your name?" "You have a beautiful child." No time for pleasantries: short, bold, and straight to the point.

That's how I was trained to "evangelize."

No matter what she says next, I am ready with an answer, a Bible verse, or a prayer. The ultimate goal, of course, is to close the deal by leading her in the "sinner's prayer,"[1] where she confesses her sins, asks forgiveness, proclaims Jesus as Lord, and invites Him into her heart. This young mom says she is already a Christian, so Mike and I move on to the next house.

---
1. Here is an example of a "sinner's prayer": "Dear God, I come to You in the name of Jesus Christ, Your Son. I believe He died on the cross for my sin. I repent of my sin, and ask You to forgive me. I believe You raised Jesus from the dead, and I receive Him now as my personal Savior and Lord. In Jesus' name I pray. Amen."

During my high school days, I prayed with many people to receive Christ and every time someone did, it was exhilarating. I am glad I was taught to share my faith. I don't regret any of those experiences. Over time, however, this method of evangelizing seemed less and less effective.

What Is Evangelism?

Since Jesus' ascension, His followers have been active in spreading the Gospel through evangelism. After all, isn't "reaching the lost" the primary duty of every Christian? Jesus said, "All authority in heaven and on earth has been given to me. Therefore go and make disciples of all nations, baptizing them in the name of the Father and of the Son and of the Holy Spirit, and teaching them to obey everything I have commanded you. And surely I am with you always, to the very end of the age" (Matthew 28:18-20).

Jesus' last words to His disciples re-emphasized the importance of evangelism, "But you will receive power when the Holy Spirit comes on you; and you will be my witnesses in Jerusalem, and in all Judea and Samaria, and to the ends of the earth" (Acts 1:8).

In obedience, Jesus' first disciples evangelized their first-century world. Through their efforts, "the Lord added to their number daily those who were being saved" (Acts 2:47). Through their preaching and influence, the first disciples introduced the Gospel to Palestine, Syria, Rome, Asia Minor, Iran, Egypt, North Africa, Armenia, Britain, India, and Ethiopia. Through their teaching and preaching, the story of Jesus went as far west as Spain. Incredibly, it has been estimated that in the first 200 years, Christianity grew from the 120 in the Upper Room (Acts 1:15) to more than one million followers. Today out of 7 billion people on earth, approximately one-third (2.3 billion), claim to be Christians. The obedience and diligence of the first disciples and the generations of disciples that followed set the table for you and me to believe.

Now it is our responsibility to evangelize our world. But what does that mean? Does it mean going door to door, or using radio, television, and the Internet? Does evangelism mean we sell everything and move to a forgotten country? What does evangelism look like in the 21st century?

Good News

The word "evangelism" is actually a transliteration[2] of the New Testament Greek word, *euaggelizo*. The first use of *euaggelizo* in the New Testament is in Matthew 4:23, "Jesus went throughout Galilee, teaching in their synagogues, preaching the *good news* of the kingdom, and healing every disease and sickness

---
2. A "transliteration" is when a word in one language is spelled with the alphabet of another language, creating a new word in the second language.

among the people."[3] The phrase, "good news" (translated "gospel" in the King James Version) is the word *euaggelizo,* or "evangelism." The most literal meaning of this word is "a proclamation of good news." The good news of the Gospel is that in and through Jesus Christ, God's kingdom has entered humankind, making people spiritually, physically, and emotionally whole.

Evangelism is proclaiming the Good News that the kingdom of God enters our reality in Jesus Christ. Jesus prayed, "Our Father in heaven, hallowed by your name, your kingdom come, your will be done on earth as it is in heaven" (Matthew 6:9-10). Evangelism is the fulfillment of that prayer. As followers of Jesus, the message we are to proclaim is that through faith in Christ, we become kingdom citizens with the task of bringing the good news of that kingdom into our homes, our neighborhoods, our work places, our churches, and our world.

The message —proclaiming the good news of the kingdom's reality through faith in Jesus—has not changed. Society has changed, but the Gospel has not. Culture has changed, but the Gospel has not. Governments have changed, but the Gospel has not. Churches have changed, but the Gospel has not. People have changed, but the Gospel has not changed nor will it ever change.

Proclaiming Good News

In Jesus' day, the word "evangelism" (*euaggelizo*) meant, in secular usage, "joyful tidings" and was used to announce birthdays of emperors. The birth of a new emperor was seen as a festive occasion for the whole world. The person proclaiming the good news was called an "evangelist" (*euangelizo*). Look in the middle of the word and you will see the word "angel." The literal meaning of "angel"[4] is "messenger." An "evangelist" is a person with a message.

In Luke chapter 1, the angel Gabriel announced the birth of Jesus to Mary saying, "Do not be afraid, Mary, you have found favor with God. You will be with child and give birth to a son, and you are to give him the name Jesus. He will be great and will be called the Son of the Most High. The Lord God will give him the throne of his father David, and he will reign over the house of Jacob forever; his kingdom will never end" (Luke 1:30-33). No doubt the announcement of the birth of the Emperor of emperors was reason to celebrate. No doubt the announcement made by Gabriel changed the world.

The word was also used to announce the victory an emperor had over his enemies. If the emperor left his kingdom in a time of war, people nervously waited for news. If the emperor conquered his foes, a messenger, or "evangelist," would

---

3. The italic indicates the Greek word, *euaggelizo*. The King James Version translates Matthew 4:23, "And Jesus went about all Galilee, teaching in their synagogues, and preaching the **gospel** of the kingdom, and healing all manner of sickness and all manner of disease among the people."

4. Like the word "evangelism," the word "angel" is a transliteration of the Greek word *aggelos*.

ride on horseback into the town proclaiming victory before the emperor returned to the city. The proclamation was good news and great cause for rejoicing! Near the end of His life on earth, Jesus rode into Jerusalem on a young colt. As He entered the town, people "began joyfully to praise God in loud voices for all the miracles they had seen: 'Blessed is the king who comes in the name of the Lord! Peace in heaven and glory in the highest!'" (Luke 19:37-38). The people saw Jesus as the conquering king returning to establish the political throne of David. Jesus, however, rode into Jerusalem as a sacrificial lamb, who would soon conquer death, hell, and the grave. Through faith in Him, people are set free from sins and empowered to live full and abundant lives. The Apostle Paul, understanding this, wrote, "In the same way, count yourselves dead to sin but alive to God in Christ Jesus. Therefore do not let sin reign in your mortal body so that you obey its evil desires. . . .Offer yourselves to God, as those who have been brought from death to life. . . .For sin shall not be your master, because you are not under law, but under grace" (Romans 6:11-14).

A third use of the word "evangelism" in first century Rome was the announcement of a new oracle, or law. The announcement of a new law was meant to be celebrated because it was believed the emperor knew what was best. Obedience to the emperor was equal with obedience to the gods.

In one of his visions while exiled on the island of Patmos, John saw three angels ("messengers"). Concerning the first angel, John said, "He had the eternal gospel[5] to proclaim to those who live on the earth—to every nation, tribe, language and people. He said in a loud voice, 'Fear God and give him glory, because the hour of his judgment has come. Worship him who made the heavens, the earth, the sea and the springs of water'" (Revelation 14:6-7). Life is better when we honor and worship Almighty God.

In the Old Testament, the idea of Gospel or good news[6] had to do with the announcement of future salvation. The best example is seen in Isaiah 52:7, "How beautiful on the mountains are the feet of those who bring good news,[7] who proclaim peace, who bring good tidings, who proclaim salvation, who say to Zion, 'Your God reigns!'" What Isaiah prophesied, Jesus fulfilled.

When we put all this together, we learn evangelism is joyfully proclaiming that the good news of salvation prophesied in the Old Testament has come to pass in Jesus the Messiah. Evangelism is joyfully proclaiming the good news that the King of kings has been born. He has defeated the enemy and set us free from

---
5. The Greek word used is *euaggelion*; the same word used in Matthew 4:23.

6. In the Septuagint (Greek translation of the Old Testament) the Hebrew word, most often translated *euaggelizo*, is *bissar*.

7. Paul quoted from Isaiah when he wrote, "How beautiful are the feet of those who bring good news" (Romans 10:15). The phrase "good news" is *euaggelizo*.

our bondage to sin. Evangelism is good news that will last forever. No wonder the Apostle Paul declared, "Oh, the depth of the riches of the wisdom and knowledge of God! How unsearchable his judgments, and his paths beyond tracing out! 'Who has known the mind of the Lord? Or who has been his counselor? Who has ever given to God, that God should repay him?' For from him and through him and to him are all things. To him be the glory forever! Amen" (Romans 11:33-36).

Evangelism in the 21st Century

On that gray Thursday afternoon when I asked that single mom if she knew if she were going to heaven or hell, what was the good news I proclaimed? How is such a confrontational question "joyful tidings"? There is no doubt it could be good news. Knowing her eternal destination could bring joy. But is asking that question really evangelism? Is there a better way to proclaim the good news that because of Jesus, God's kingdom is a present reality?

Evangelism in the 21st century is no different—and yet extremely different—than any other time of history. The one constant is Jesus. He is the centerpiece of the Gospel. Jesus is the Good News. Jesus has appeared, He continues to appear, and He will appear again. Any time Jesus appears—past, present, and future—God's kingdom appears with Him.

This is very good news!

Jesus Has Appeared

God created us to have a relationship with us. But first the bad news: *Sin has separated us from God, and no amount of goodness on our part can bridge the chasm between us and God.* God made you in His image (Genesis 1:27). We were meant to be whole and complete. The very first consequence of sin is separation from God (Genesis 3:21-24). Because of sin, we are separated and no longer whole.

Through the Law and the Prophets, God wanted to demonstrate that on our own, through keeping rules, we can be good, but we can never be good enough. We can be moral, but we can't be made whole again. We can't be perfect. The purpose of the Law was never to put us back together, bringing us back into relationship with God. The Law showed how broken we really were. Paul said the Law was a curse (Galatians 3:10). The Law was not good news. Keeping the Law was not evangelism.

The good news is Jesus. Jesus "redeemed us from the curse of the law by becoming a curse for us" (Galatians 3:13). The purpose of the Law was to "lead us to Christ that we might be justified by faith" (Galatians 3:24). It's called grace; and the same grace that appeared to the first disciples continues to appear today. Paul wrote, "For the grace of God that brings salvation has appeared to all men" (Titus 2:11).

The fact that grace *has* come and Jesus *has* appeared is what makes evangelism possible. Grace cannot be earned; grace is a gift. Paul wrote, "For it is by grace you have been saved, through faith—and this not from yourselves, it is the gift of God—not by works, so that no one can boast" (Ephesians 2:8-9). "Salvation," being brought back into relationship with God, cannot be achieved through rules; it can only be received as a gift of grace. That's good news! Sharing that news with others is evangelism!

But the good news gets even better. If salvation were only about heaven, that would be significant. But there is more. God's grace, received through faith in Jesus, gives us the strength we need to live in the here and now. The grace of God "teaches us to say 'No' to ungodliness and worldly passions, and to live self-controlled, upright and godly lives in this present age" (Titus 2:12).

My question to the single mom about the afterlife was short-sighted. I should have asked: "Would you like to know, right now, how you can be a better mom to your children?" "Would you like to know, right now, how you can live a fuller, more abundant life?" "Did you know there is a way, right now, for you to live a life others only dream about?" "Did you know that right now, at this very moment, God wants to break into your reality?"

God's grace, received in Jesus, has as much to do with the here and now as it does the hereafter. This is why it is called evangelism. This is why it is very good news.

Grace gives us the strength not to do what God does not want us to do ("ungodliness") and to not do what our human lusts would rather us do ("worldly passions"). Think about it: many times, what gives people the most trouble is being disobedient to God and obedient to themselves. We make a mess of our lives because we very seldom say "yes" to God, and we hardly ever say "no" to ourselves. God, through Jesus, wants to change that.

Grace not only gives us strength to deny but also strength to affirm lives characterized by discipline ("self-controlled"), integrity ("upright") and godliness ("godly lives"). How much better would our world be if we were known as people who did what we said we were going to do, treated others the way we wanted to be treated, and placed God first in every facet of our lives? Evangelism is the good news that life can be lived in the here and now, above the fray and chaos of most everyone else.

Jesus Will Appear

The fact that grace *continues* to come and Jesus *will* appear is what makes evangelism necessary. This present life is preparation for eternal life. As important as this life is, there is more to life than this. God's grace, received by faith in Jesus, makes this life endurable "while we wait for the blessed hope—the glorious appearing of our great God and Savior, Jesus Christ" (Titus 2:13).

In the Bible, "waiting" is active, not passive. The King James Version reads, "Looking for that blessed hope." While we are waiting, we are to be looking. While we are waiting, God is working deep within us. While we are waiting, God is working diligently around us. God says, "Be still, and know that I am God; I will be exalted among the nations, I will be exalted in the earth" (Psalm 46:10). More specifically, according to Paul, while we are waiting, we are to be living a life of hope as we wait for the Hope. A better word for "hope" is "expectation." When the New Testament talks about hope, it refers to something that will definitely come to pass. We are not hoping Jesus returns. Our hope is that He will return.

Furthermore, our hope is based on fact, not fantasy. The fact is, Jesus "gave himself for us to redeem us from all wickedness and to purify for himself a people that are his very own, eager to do what is good" (Titus 2:14). Apart from Jesus, we are still separated from God and enslaved to wickedness. Through His sacrificial death, Jesus paid our ransom and God forgave our sins. Now we belong to Him. We have eternal life, and eternity starts now as we "do what is good," bringing God's kingdom (of which we are citizens) into our present reality.

This is very good news. This is evangelism.

Wrap Up

What does evangelism look like in the 21st century?

It looks like it did in the first century. The world of the first disciples was full of idolatry, political corruption, and gross immorality. Yet that is the world into which Jesus came, and the church was born. Our society needs good news! Your neighbors and co-workers need good news! We have that good news and it is time to start proclaiming that through Jesus Christ, God's kingdom has broken into our existence.

What does evangelism look like in the 21st century? First, evangelism must be bold. The word "evangelism" means a proclamation, and it is a bold proclamation. Not the type of boldness it takes for a teenager to knock on a stranger's door on a Thursday afternoon, but the type of boldness that is willing to sacrifice everything for the Gospel. The Apostle Paul wrote, "I am not ashamed of the gospel, because it is the power of God for the salvation of everyone who believes: first for the Jew, then for the Gentile" (Romans 1:16).

Second, in the 21st century, evangelism must offer hope. If people were honest, they would tell you their perception of hell isn't any worse than what they experience every day. People need hope—not of a better life to come, but of a more tolerable life now. If the Gospel does not bring hope today, then it is not really good news. In Christ there is hope for the present as well as the future. By the way you've lived your life, when was the last time someone asked you to give a reason for the hope you have (1 Peter 3:15)? If we are not offering hope, we are not evangelizing.

Third, evangelism must be genuine. People need to see a real difference in their lives. Not a different list of do's and don'ts, but a difference in quality, values, and peace. Society is full of people who claim to be Christians but whose lives argue against that claim. Genuine belief attracts people to Jesus. Hypocrisy repels them.

Fourth, 21st-century evangelism will look like relationships. Yes, there is a time to confront people with the Gospel. But confrontation from a friend is far more effective than confrontation from a stranger. Christianity is relationship-driven, not rule-driven. We see this in God's relationship with Himself, as witnessed in the Trinity: our relationship with Jesus, our relationship with other believers, and our relationship with non-believers. People need to know you love them, even when they reject Christ.

Finally, evangelism in the 21st century must emphasize wholeness. Evangelism is the good news that in Christ, a person can be made whole again. Jesus' offer of salvation is all-encompassing. He has come to save people spiritually, physically, and emotionally.

What better news is there than to proclaim with Jesus, "The time has come.... The kingdom of God is near. Repent and believe the good news!" (Mark 1:15).

Keys to Chapter One:
- The definition of evangelism is as follows: *Evangelism is proclaiming the good news that the kingdom of God enters our reality through Jesus Christ.*
  - ❖ Evangelism is joyfully proclaiming the good news that the King of kings has been born.
  - ❖ He has defeated the enemy and set us free from our sin bondage.
  - ❖ Evangelism is good news that will last forever.
- Evangelism in the 21st century is no different, and yet extremely different, than any other time of history.
- Evangelism is possible because grace has come and Jesus has appeared.

- Evangelism is necessary because grace continues to come and Jesus will, once again, appear.
- The good news is that any time Jesus appears—past, present, and future—God's kingdom appears with Him.
- When the New Testament talks about hope, it refers to something that will definitely come to pass. We are not hoping Jesus returns. Our hope is that He will return.
- Five words that describe what evangelism in the 21st century will look like are: (1) Boldness, (2) Hope, (3) Genuineness, (4) Relational, (5) Wholeness.

Questions for Discussion:
1. Do you remember when you accepted Jesus into your life? What were the circumstances surrounding that decision? Who was instrumental in evangelizing you?
2. Have you ever attempted to evangelize another person? What was that experience like? What was the circumstance? What was the result? What did you learn?
3. When you hear the word "evangelism," what immediately comes to mind? Is your initial reaction positive or negative? Why?
4. Discuss the different usages of the word "evangelism" in Jesus' day. How would you apply each usage in sharing the Gospel today?
5. Of the five words that describe evangelism in the 21st century, which one do you think is most important? Why did you choose that one? If you were to place these five words in order, from most important to least, in what order would you place them? Explain.

2
Evangelism and the Kingdom of God

"Oorah!"
"Hooah!"
"Hooyah!"

Are you familiar with those three words? Yes, they are real words. . . .or at least real sayings.

These three words, or sayings, are battle cries, or rallying cries, or cries of acknowledgment for the United States military. All three words basically mean the same thing and are used to build teamwork, lift morale, and motivate soldiers. While meaning the same thing, however, each word is used exclusively by different branches of the military.

"Oorah!" (pronounced, "ooh-rah") is used by the United States Marine Corps. A more commonly known USMC rallying cry is *"Semper Fidelis"* (or simply, "semper fi"), which is Latin for "always faithful" or "always loyal." A strong sense of camaraderie is established when soldiers yell these community words.

"Hooah!" (pronounced, "hu-a") is used by the United States Army and the United States Air Force. When this word is said in unison, you can feel the electricity in the air.

"Hooyah!" (pronounced, "hu-ya") is used by the United States Navy, especially the Navy SEALs and the Navy Deep Sea Divers. Hearing a group of sailors say these word in deep, bass voices, makes the hairs stand up on the back of your neck.

Battle cries have existed since the beginning of warfare. They instill a sense of pride and honor, reminding warriors why they are fighting. In modern times, battle cries have morphed into slogans, bumper stickers, and sound bites. Common expressions have a way of bringing unique individuals together ... if only for a moment.

What does this have to do with evangelism in the 21st century?

Anticipation

By the end of the Old Testament period, an expectation that the Messiah would soon come started to grow among the Jewish people. During the four hundred years between the close of the Old Testament and the beginning of the New Testament, the anticipation of the coming Messiah reached a fever pitch. As a result, during this time, known as the Intertestamental Period[1], a rallying cry, of sorts, became popular. In Hebrew, that rallying cry was *"malkuth ha shamayim."*[2]

Malkuth ha shamayim. Say it out loud, *malkuth ha shamayim*. It rolls off the tongue, does it not? I have no idea how it is really pronounced so your enunciation is as good as mine.

What does this Hebrew phrase mean? It is difficult to translate, but the basic idea is "'the sole sovereignty of God,' the recognition that God alone has the right to rule and dominate the life and affairs ... of the world. *Malkuth ha shamayim* was a fundamental tenet of Judaism, based on ... the first commandment to Moses at Sinai: '[Y]ou shall have no other gods before me' (Exodus 20:3)."[3]

This idea, that God alone is sovereign, carried at least three meanings in the Old Testament: (1) God as King of the universe. (Psalm 47—"Clap your hands, all you nations; shout to God with cries of joy. How awesome is the LORD Most High, the great King over all the earth! ... For God is the King of all the earth.... God reigns over the nations ... for the kings of the earth belong to God; he is greatly exalted.") (2) God as the sole King of Israel. (Isaiah 41:21—"'Present your case,' says the LORD. 'Set forth your arguments,' says Jacob's King.") (3) God as King in the future sense. (Psalm 146:10—"The LORD reigns forever, your God, O Zion, for all generations.")[4]

The fact that God alone was to reign is why Israel refused to bow to earthly kings and as a result was forced into bondage. It is why they hesitated in having their own king—relying on "judges" instead. (The Old Testament judges were more like "freedom fighters" than they were judicial rulers.) *Malkuth ha sha-*

---

1. This period, also known as the "silent years" because there were no prophets and God seemed quiet, covers from approximately the end of Malachi's prophecies (420 B.C.) to the birth of Jesus (around 7–5 B.C.).

2. I am indebted to Dr. Obery M. Hendricks, Jr. and his treatment and explanation of *malkuth ha shamayim* in his book, *The Politics of Jesus*. Dr. Hendricks discusses the significance of *malkuth ha shamayim* in chapter one of his book, especially pages 19–21.

3. Obery M. Hendricks, Jr. *The Politics of Jesus* (New York: Doubleday, 2006), 19.

4. Ibid.

mayim is also why Samuel reacted so harshly when the Israelites asked for their own earthly king. The Bible says, "But when they said, 'Give us a king to lead us,' this displeased Samuel; so he prayed to the Lord. And the Lord told him: 'Listen to all that the people are saying to you; it is not you they have rejected, but they have rejected me as their king'" (1 Samuel 8:6-7).

Outside of King David, and one or two others, all of Israel's kings were failures. Life did not go well for the Hebrews when they were ruled by earthly kings. Eventually, the ten tribes would be exiled to Assyria, and when that empire fell, the remaining two tribes would be exiled to Babylon.[5] For this reason, much of the Old Testament prophecies had to do with the coming of *Mashiach* ("Messiah"— the "anointed one"). The most famous of these prophecies was from Isaiah 61:1-2, "The Spirit of the Sovereign Lord is on me, because the Lord has anointed me to preach good news to the poor. He has sent me to bind up the brokenhearted ... to proclaim the year of the Lord's favor."

As anticipation grew of the coming Messiah, exactly what the Messiah would do when He arrived changed. No longer was the Messiah seen as a spiritual redeemer; slowly He became a political figure. It was believed when the Messiah came He would overthrow the Jewish oppressors and reestablish the throne of David. Thus, the Messiah would be the ultimate "freedom fighter" bringing with Him *malkuth ha shamayim*.

A forerunner of the anticipated messianic revolution was the Maccabean Revolt.

Around 167 B.C., the Greek occupiers issued an edict that all Jews recognize Antiochus IV (the Roman Emperor) as *Epiphanes* (meaning "god manifest"), swearing allegiance to him. When soldiers entered a small village to enforce the orders, an outraged Jewish peasant named Mattathias invoked *malkuth ha shamayim,* saying, "Although all the Gentiles in the king's realm obey him, so that they forsake the religion of their ancestors ... *[w]e will not obey the words of the king ...*"[6]

After his death, Mattathias's son, Judas Maccabeus, led the guerilla war and reconsecrated the temple in Jerusalem. The Jewish festival of Hanukkah (which means "rededication") celebrates this victory. As time went on, the expectation that the Messiah would soon come reached a fever pitch.

Leading up to the announcement of Jesus, several people claimed to be the Messiah, and several revolts against the Romans occurred. For example, between 63 and 37 B.C., approximately 150,000 Palestinians were killed by the Roman

---

5. Sometime after the reign of King David, the nation of Israel split in two with ten tribes going to the north, becoming Israel, and two tribes going to south, becoming Judah. Babylon is in present-day Iraq, near the city of Baghdad.

6. First Maccabees 2:19, 22 (NABRE), italics mine.

authorities in revolutionary uprisings. Another skirmish that happened around A.D. 6 is mentioned by Gamaliel in Acts 5:35-39, "Men of Israel, consider carefully what you intend to do to these men. Some time ago Theudas appeared, claiming to be somebody, and about four hundred men rallied to him. He was killed, all his followers were dispersed, and it all came to nothing. After him Judas the Galilean appeared in the days of the census and led a band of people in revolt. He too was killed, and all his followers were scattered. Therefore, in the present case I advise you: Leave these men alone! Let them go! For if their purpose or activity is of human origin, it will fail. But if it is from God, you will not be able to stop these men; you will only find yourselves fighting against God."[7]

Now, fast forward to the day Jesus walked into His hometown synagogue, was handed the scroll of the prophet Isaiah, and asked to read. The assigned passage for that day was Isaiah's prophecy about the coming Messiah (Isaiah 61:1-2). The people would know this prophecy by heart; just reading it would bring excitement; Jesus would be "preaching to the choir"; this was everyone's favorite prophecy. Jesus read, "The Spirit of the Lord is on me, because he has anointed me to preach the good news to the poor. He has sent me to proclaim freedom for the prisoners and recovery of sight for the blind, to release the oppressed, to proclaim the year of the Lord's favor" (Luke 4:18-19).

Then Jesus did something totally unexpected. Dramatically, He rolled up the scroll, handed it back to the attendant, sat down, and said, "Today this scripture is fulfilled in your hearing" (v. 21).

How did the people, who were anticipating God sending His Messiah, react? Were they excited? Did they embrace Jesus' words? Did they applaud? Were they ready to give up everything and follow Him?

NO!

The Bible says, "All the people in the synagogue were furious when they heard this. They got up, drove him out of the town, and took him to the brow of the hill on which the town was built, in order to throw him down the cliff" (vv. 28-29).

Utterly amazing!

Absolutely predictable!

Some Questions to Consider

I assume you are reading this book because you are interested in evangelism. You are anticipating God moving in your lives, and the lives of others. You love seeing God draw people far from Him into a deep relationship with Himself. You desire to see God reign in your life. You have been praying for God to show up. When God does, don't be like Jesus' audience and move from anticipation and expectation to rejection and disappointment.

---

7. More than likely, Theudas claimed to be the Messiah, and that is what got him killed. The "men" referred to is Peter and the other apostles who had appeared for questioning in front of the Sanhedrin.

Allow me to stop and ask three questions (with several sub-questions) by way of application:

Question #1: *What are you anticipating God to do?*
Do you live your life with the reality that God is still active and involved in the affairs of men? Do you believe He wants to be involved in your personal affairs? Do you anticipate that God loves you and will take care of you? Do you believe He loves other people and does not want anyone to perish for eternity apart from Him (2 Peter 3:9)? Do you live with an expectation that, once again, Jesus is going to break into the world, and it could happen at any moment? What are you anticipating God to do?

Question #2: *How would you react if God did what you anticipated but not like you expected?*
Would you be disappointed? Would you embrace Him? Would you reject Him?

The reason most people in Jesus' day rejected Him as the Messiah was not because they were not anticipating a Messiah, but because the Messiah they got was not the Messiah they expected. Likewise, the reason most people reject Jesus today is not because they don't think they are sinners in need of grace and forgiveness, but because the Savior (grace and forgiveness) they get is not the type of Savior (grace and forgiveness) they expected. Accepting Jesus is both easy and difficult. Giving your life to Christ is simple and complex at the same time.

One more question:

Question #3: *In your anticipation of what you are expecting God to do, are you missing what God is already doing?*
God is at work at all times, all around you. Even when He seems quiet, He is still actively engaged in what is going on. In fact, the more distant and silent God seems, the nearer and most active He really is.

Back to the Story

Malkuth ha shamayim is important because the Israelites believed the Messiah would announce His entrance into the world by proclaiming, *"Malkuth ha shamayim";* and Jesus did not do that, or did He?

Remember, the phrase *malkuth ha shamayim* is difficult to translate? The idea behind the phrase is the sole sovereignty of God. But among the Jews, leading up to the time of Jesus, the phrase came to mean **the kingdom of God,** or, **the kingdom of heaven.** Jesus loudly proclaimed *malkuth ha shamayim* when He boldly said, "The **kingdom of God** is near" (Mark 1:15, emphasis mine). The idea behind the word "near" is "at hand" or "approaching." Jesus was announcing that He was the Messiah and that in Him the anointed One of God had arrived. With His arrival came *malkuth ha shamayim,* the sole sovereignty of God, the kingdom of heaven. The people understood Jesus was claiming to be God, and to them it was blasphemy, and blasphemy was punishable by death. Therefore, they wanted to throw Him over a cliff.

Malkuth ha shamayim Is Evangelism

According to Mark's Gospel, this announcement that God's kingdom becomes a reality in Jesus. *Malkuth ha shamayim* is "good news." In other words, evangelism is proclaiming *malkuth ha shamayim* has arrived in Christ Jesus. You cannot separate evangelism from God's kingdom. You cannot understand evangelism without understanding the meaning and the implication of the kingdom of God. Jesus said, "The kingdom of God is near. Repent and believe the good news!" (Mark 1:15). All of Jesus' teachings, all of His healings, and all of His miracles, were demonstrations of God's kingdom in the here and now. Then, when He left this world, Jesus gave all His authority to bring the kingdom of God into existence, and to demonstrate the present reality of God's kingdom, to His followers. Jesus said, "I tell you the truth, anyone who has faith in me will do what I have been doing. He will do even greater things than these, because I am going to the Father" (John 14:12).

Wherever Jesus' followers are, there the kingdom of God is near or at hand. This is evangelism. If you are a follower of Jesus, wherever you go, you take God's kingdom with you. This is what it means to evangelize. At times, God's kingdom shows up in the spectacular, and supernatural things occur—healings, miracles, and restorations. At other times, His kingdom shows up in the silence . . . and supernatural things occur—forgiveness, peace, encouragement. Evangelism, then, is not a program in the church. Evangelism is the very essence of what it means to be a disciple of Jesus, being the body of Jesus, His hands and feet, in this present day. Evangelism is Jesus' followers being the incarnation of God in their present reality.

The Now and Not Yet of the Kingdom

Jesus clearly proclaimed He was the Messiah and with Him came God's kingdom. His proclamation is the heart of evangelism. But while the kingdom of God is a present reality, it is also a future hope. Thus, God's kingdom is both now and not yet.

The moment a person "repents and believes the good news" that Jesus is the Messiah (*malkuth ha shamayim*), at that very moment that person enters God's kingdom and has all the rights of full citizenship.

What are those rights?

What does life in God's kingdom look like?

Well, the prophecy of Isaiah which Jesus read mentions several rights, or characteristics of the kingdom. First, in God's kingdom there is justice for the poor. Jesus said, "The Spirit of the Lord is on me, because he has anointed me to preach good news to the poor" (Luke 4:18a). In our society, the poor are neglected, overlooked, and mistreated. But in the kingdom of heaven, "the last will be first, and the first will be last" (Matthew 20:16). For the "poor" (literally and figuratively), Jesus offers hope and security. When we stand up for justice and defend the most vulnerable in our society, we are bringing God's kingdom into our existence, and that is evangelism.

Next, in God's kingdom there is freedom for the imprisoned (Luke 4:18b). All over the world people are wrongly imprisoned, but in God's kingdom, even the justice system will be just and fair and right. Furthermore, in God's kingdom, even those who are rightly incarcerated experience a newfound freedom in Christ. People everywhere are also imprisoned by their addictive behavior, bad habits, and harmful emotions. In God's kingdom, all are set free because all have been forgiven.

Furthermore, citizens of God's kingdom have the right to be physically healed, emotionally whole, and spiritually alive (v. 18c). If you read the Gospels carefully, you notice all of Jesus' healings had to do with making people whole again physically, emotionally, and spiritually. In Jesus Christ, whatever healing a person needs is available—if not in this life, definitely in the life to come.

Jesus concluded His synagogue reading with Isaiah's words, "to proclaim the year of the Lord's favor" (v. 19). According to Leviticus 25:8-13, every fiftieth year was to be set aside as a "Year of Jubilee." This is what Isaiah, and Jesus, had in mind by "the year of the Lord's favor." During the Year of Jubilee, land was returned to the original owners, debts were forgiven, and slaves were set free. Every fifty years, everything was once again made right. Over time, the Year of Jubilee came to mean the time of God's future salvation, the time when God's kingdom will be fully and completely realized on earth, the time when God will be sovereign over all. That time is not yet here, but it is near and it is nearing. We see glimpses of it every day, and it is coming soon.

Thus, while right now we see glimpses of God's kingdom through justice, freedom, healing, wholeness, and life; we are "aliens and strangers in the world" (1 Peter 2:11); this present world is not the kingdom of heaven. But in the same way that Jesus came once proclaiming God's kingdom was at hand, He will come again, bringing that kingdom to fruition.

In the meantime, we, His followers, are stewards of the message that in Christ, God's kingdom is near. It is in proclaiming this message that we evangelize because it is this message that is good news.

Personal Evangelism

However, before you can evangelize, you must first be evangelized. Before you can experience God's kingdom, you must first become a citizen of His kingdom. How?

Jesus tells us how to become citizens of God's kingdom when He says, "Repent and believe" (Mark 1:15). To "repent" means to change the direction of your life by changing your attitude toward the things of God. Repentance is a change that leads to action. The action repentance leads to is "belief," which carries the idea of entrusting your life in that which you believe. Here, Jesus says to change your life by changing what you thought about God and entrusting yourself in the belief that Jesus is the Messiah.

We need to repent because we have been trying to build our own kingdoms. We need to repent because we have tried to colonize Jesus into our kingdom instead of crossing over the border into His. We need to repent because our anticipation and expectations have not lined up with who Jesus is and what He wants to accomplish. We need to repent because we have been illegal immigrants in God's kingdom. We have entered by our own rules and have tried to take advantage of all the privilege without sharing the responsibility. We believe Jesus is coming when what we need to do is live like He is already here. We need to repent because we have not believed in the present reality of His kingdom, and we have not been motivated to proclaim the good news of His kingdom to others. Instead of transforming our world, we have tried to endure our world, or conform to our world, because we know that one day—in the future—there's a better day coming. Jesus said the better day coming is already here and available to all who will repent and believe.

Keys to Chapter Two:
- The most literal translation of *malkuth ha shamayim* is the sole sovereignty of God. However, the phrase came to mean "the kingdom of God" or "the kingdom of heaven" and was a rallying cry for Jews expecting a political ("freedom fighter") type of Messiah. The phrase carried three meanings in the Old Testament.

    1. God as King of the universe.

    2. God as the sole King of Israel.

    3. God as King in the future sense.

- Evangelism is Jesus' followers being the incarnation of God in their present reality.

- You cannot understand evangelism without first understanding the importance of the implications of the kingdom of God.

- Accepting Jesus is both easy and difficult. Giving your life to Christ is simple and complex at the same time.
- As a follower of Jesus, wherever you go, you take God's kingdom with you.
- The kingdom of God is both a present reality and a future hope. The kingdom of God is both now and not yet.
- You become a citizen of God's kingdom through repentance and belief.

Questions for Discussion:
1. How would you explain to someone else the "sole sovereignty of God"? How important do you think it is for God to have sole sovereignty over your life?
2. Why do you think the people in Jesus' hometown reacted so strongly to Jesus' claim to be the Messiah prophesied by Isaiah?
3. What are some specific things you would like to see God do in your life and the lives of those you know and love? (Be as specific as possible.)
4. Can you think of a time in your life when God did what you asked but not in the way you expected? Describe the situation. How did you respond?
5. When did you become a citizen of God's kingdom? What were the circumstances that brought you to a place of repentance and belief?

3
Evangelism in the Early Church

Of all Jesus' disciples, I relate to Peter the most.[1]
Born around 6 B.C. in Bethsaida[2], a small fishing village on the banks of the Sea of Galilee and the Jordan River, Peter grew up learning Greek, Aramaic, and Hebrew. His father's name was Jonah (or John). According to the Jewish custom of the day, Peter went to school at the local synagogue from age six to thirteen. Following his formal education, he went to work as a commercial fisherman and was apparently very successful.[3]

I like to fish, I love the water, and I am more comfortable around blue-collar people (like fishermen) than white-collar people. I relate to Peter because we have similar interests.

Peter had a reputation for being rough, opinionated, and abrasive. (I have been accused of all three.) Whatever he did, he did it 100 percent. (That's what I try to do.) Peter was stubborn; he didn't let anyone or anything keep him from doing what he wanted. (Guilty!) While those traits helped Peter build a successful fishing business, they did not endear him to others. Yet, in spite of his callous exterior, Peter had a big heart—big enough for Jesus to choose him to be first among the disciples and the first leader of the church.

---

1. In the Gospels, Peter is known by three names: Simon, Peter, and Cephas. "Simon" was his Hebrew birth name. "Peter" and "Cephas" both mean "rock," referring to the nickname given to him by Jesus. "Peter" is Greek, and "Cephas" is Aramaic.

2. Pronounced *beth-sa-e-de*. The name means either "house of fishing" or "fisherman's haven." Both possibilities tell what the town was best known for.

3. What did Peter look like? In 1968, Pope Paul VI declared that the bones kept in Rome, said to be Peter's, were actually Peter's. According to archaeologists who have studied those bones, Peter was a stocky, muscular man, about 5'4" tall. Most early representations show him to have a fair complexion, curly hair, and a curly beard.

From Caesarea to Pentecost

Peter's brother, Andrew, introduced him to Jesus (John 1:40-42). Jesus quickly nicknamed him "Cephas," which is Aramaic for "rock" (v. 42). Later, while walking to the town of Caesarea Philippi, Jesus asked, "Who do people say the Son of Man is?" (Matthew 16:13). The disciples told Jesus what they heard—the things others said about Him. Jesus then got personal and asked, "Who do you say I am?" (v. 15). Peter, who had a tendency to speak—sometimes without thinking—answered, "You are the Christ, the Son of the living God" (v. 16). This time his quick-shooting mouth was right on target.

"Christ" was not Jesus' last name. "Christ" is the Greek word for "Messiah" or "Anointed One." Peter was professing that Jesus was the Promised One of God prophesied about in the Old Testament. Peter was professing that Jesus was God, and with Him came *malkuth ha shamayim*.

Another important word in Matthew 16:16 is the word "the." In the Greek language, the article "the" can be used to denote exclusivity. Peter, in essence, was saying, "You are *the one and only* Christ, *the one and only* Son of *the one and only* living God."

Peter's answer was not simply a statement of faith. It was (and is) the foundational statement of what it means to follow Jesus. His statement encompasses all of who Jesus is, what He came to earth to do, and how His presence in the world brought about the kingdom of God, changing everything.

We know this to be true because of the way Jesus responded. He said, "Blessed are you, Simon son of Jonah, for this was not revealed to you by man, but by my Father in heaven. And I tell you that you are Peter, and on this rock I will build my church, and the gates of Hades will not overcome it" (vv. 17-18). Peter's confession is the "rock," the cornerstone, on which the church is built, and the way the church is built is through evangelism.

The Birth of the Church

Throughout Jesus' ministry, Peter stumbled and grew, stumbled again and matured, and stumbled some more and grew some more. He reached a low point by denying Jesus when Jesus needed him most (see Matthew 26:69-75). While sitting on an early morning beach eating fish for breakfast after His resurrection, Jesus forgave Peter and reinstated him to his rightful place of leadership (see John 21).

Forty days later, after another meal with Jesus and the other disciples, this time in Jerusalem, Jesus speaks once more, saying, "Do not leave Jerusalem, but wait for the gift my Father promised, which you have heard me speak about. . . . But you will receive power when the Holy Spirit comes on you; and you will be my witnesses in Jerusalem, and in all Judea and Samaria, and to the ends of the earth" (Acts 1:4, 8). Then, right before their eyes, Jesus ascended into heaven. Immediately, Peter took charge and Matthias was elected as a disciple in place of Judas (v. 26). In obedience to Jesus' words, they went to a house in Jerusalem and waited. And waited. And waited.

"Suddenly a sound like the blowing of a violent wind came from heaven and filled the whole house where they were sitting. They saw what seemed to be tongues of fire that separated and came to rest on each of them. All of them were filled with the Holy Spirit and began to speak in other tongues as the Spirit enabled them" (2:2-4).

As soon as the waiting was over, the church was born!

Peter's First Sermon

People in the surrounding neighborhood heard the commotion coming from inside the house and gathered outside. The crowd was ethnically diverse, but everyone heard the disciples speaking in their own language. Some people were amazed at what they heard and witnessed, while others ridiculed and criticized. A large crowd (apparently in the thousands) gathered, and Peter stood up and preached his very first sermon and the very first sermon of the church (Acts 2:14-41).

Evangelism Principles from the Early Church

Often, if you want to know how things *should* be done, you go back to how things *were* originally done. That principle hold true here. The church doesn't need more gimmicks and newer programs. What we need is a return to the model given to us by Peter and the early church. From Peter's first sermon and the example of the church in the Book of Acts, we learn several principles for evangelism in any place and any era.

Holy Spirit Empowered and Directed

The disciples were told not to leave Jerusalem but wait for the Holy Spirit (Acts 1:4-5). They were promised that the Spirit would empower and enable them to "be my witnesses" (v. 8). As soon as the disciples "were filled with the Holy Spirit," they began to proclaim the wonders of God in ways everyone could understand "as the Spirit enabled them" (2:4).

This dependence on the Holy Spirit was not a one-time thing but continued throughout the story of Acts. Consider the following:

- One of the strongest statements Peter made was before the Jewish court called the Sanhedrin. Peter said, "Salvation is found in no one else, for there is no other name under heaven given to men by which we must be saved" (4:12). This statement was made only after Peter had been "filled with the Holy Spirit" (v. 8).

- In Acts 8:26-40, Philip was directed by "an angel of the Lord" (v. 26) to go south toward Gaza. Along the way, he met an Ethiopian eunuch who was reading the prophet Isaiah. The Bible then reads, "The **Spirit told** Philip, 'Go to that chariot...'" (v. 29, emphasis mine). Philip obeyed and explained the prophecy about a suffering Servant to the eunuch. The eunuch believed and was baptized. "When they came up out of the water, the Spirit of the Lord suddenly took Philip away, and the eunuch did not see him again, but went on his way rejoicing" (v. 39).

- In Acts 10:9-48, while praying on a rooftop, Peter had a vision that convinced him of his own prejudice toward people who were different from him. At the same time he was receiving this vision, a Roman soldier named Cornelius was looking for him (vv. 1-8). "While Peter was still thinking about the vision, **the Spirit said** to him, 'Simon, three men are looking for you. So get up and go downstairs. Do not hesitate to go with them for I have sent them'" (vv. 19-20, emphasis mine). Peter went with the men to Cornelius's house; confessed his sin of racism to them (v. 28); told them "the good news of peace through Jesus Christ, who is Lord of all" (v. 36);[4] and told them the story and meaning of Jesus' life, death, and resurrection. Cornelius and many others believed, were filled with the Holy Spirit, and were baptized. Peter then explained these events to the apostles, emphasizing that he only did what the Spirit had directed and empowered him to do (11:12).

- In Acts 16:6-10, Paul wanted to go to the province of Asia and the city of Bithynia, but the Holy Spirit prevented him from going in that direction. Instead, Paul had a vision to travel to Macedonia and preach the Gospel there, convinced this was the direction the Holy Spirit was sending them.

The principle is clear: *Evangelism in the 21st century will continue to be empowered and directed by the Holy Spirit.* In fact, apart from the presence and power of the Holy Spirit, evangelism and life change cannot take place. The very first place to start any evangelism effort is to go to your upper room, pray, and wait for the Holy Spirit to lead, guide, empower, and direct.

How long do you wait? As long as necessary. We are impatient people and

---
4. The Greek word translated "good news" is the word from which we get our English word, "evangelism."

waiting is hard to do. God said, "Be still, and know that I am God" (Psalm 46:10). Waiting is easier once you recognize that God is in the waiting.

How do we know when it is time to move forward? There is no easy answer to that question except to say you will know when you know. God will show up. He will reveal Himself, and there will be no mistake it is He. Jesus said, "My sheep hear My voice, and I know them, and they follow Me" (John 10:27 NKJV).

Rooted in Scripture

The example of rooting evangelism in Scripture goes back to Jesus Himself. He used Isaiah to announce His messianic ministry (Luke 4:14-30). Then, after His resurrection, while walking on the road to Emmaus with Cleopas and one other person, "And beginning with Moses and all the Prophets, he explained to them what was said in all the Scriptures concerning himself" (24:27).

Following Jesus' example, after receiving the Holy Spirit and drawing a large crowd on the Day of Pentecost (Acts 2), Peter stood up to preach, saying, "This is what was spoken by the prophet Joel" (v. 16). In addition to the prophet Joel, Peter also quoted David (vv. 25-28, 34-35).

In his conversation with the Ethiopian eunuch, Philip used the passage in Isaiah that the eunuch was already reading and "began with that very passage of Scripture and told him the good news about Jesus" (8:35). James (Jesus' brother) used the Old Testament at the Jerusalem Council to conclude they should make it as easy as possible for Gentiles to follow God (15:15-19).

The good news we are to proclaim is all about what God promised and prophesied in Scripture about the coming Messiah and the kingdom of God. *Effective evangelism must root itself in the teachings of Scripture*, not the newest trend, the next great idea, or the most recent pop-culture, feel-good-in-the-moment motivational speech. Evangelism is the good news that the kingdom of God has become a reality in Jesus Christ. It's about Him, not us. It's about Jesus, not numerical growth. It's about salvation, nothing more and nothing less.

Centered on Jesus Christ

Talk of anything other than Jesus and calls for commitment to anything other than Jesus is not evangelism, nor is it good news. You are not the center of evangelism and neither is your church. *Real evangelism is always centered on the life, death, resurrection, and work of Jesus Christ.* The goal of evangelism is to point people to Jesus. It is in Him that God's kingdom resides.

Peter's first sermon focused entirely on Jesus. Peter preached, "Men of Israel, listen to this: Jesus of Nazareth was a man accredited by God to you by miracles, wonders and signs, which God did among you through him, as you yourselves know. This man was handed over to you by God's set purpose and foreknowledge; and you, with the help of wicked men, put him to death by nailing him to the cross. But God raised him from the dead, freeing him from the agony of death, because it was impossible for death to keep its hold on him" (Acts 2:22-24).

Later in his sermon, Peter continued, "God has raised this Jesus to life, and we are all witnesses of the fact. Exalted to the right hand of God, he has received from the Father the promised Holy Spirit and has poured out what you now see and hear.... Therefore let all Israel be assured of this: God has made this Jesus, whom you crucified, both Lord and Christ" (vv. 32-33, 36).

Stressed Repentance and Forgiveness

Peter's sermon pricked the very heart of his hearers. Out of deep conviction the people asked, "Brothers, what shall we do?" (v. 37).

"Peter replied, 'Repent and be baptized, every one of you, in the name of Jesus Christ for the forgiveness of your sins'" (v. 38).

After His baptism, Jesus announced His ministry and then called for people to "repent and believe the good news!" (Mark 1:15). Now, after explaining the purpose and ministry of Jesus to the crowd, Peter makes the same call to "repent." *Evangelism is about Jesus and His desire and ability to forgive sins. However, sins are not forgiven until you repent!* Jesus did not come to make good people better. Jesus came to forgive sins. He came to make wicked people whole and evil people righteous. Anything less than stressing our need for repentance and forgiveness fails to communicate the real message of Jesus.

To "repent" means to change your mind and your very purpose for living. *Repentance involves a turning away from sin and turning to faith in Jesus.* Repentance is a change of attitude about sin, God, selfishness, and righteousness that results in a change of lifestyle. One of the first characteristics of this change is the willingness to make your new faith in Jesus public through baptism (Acts 2:38). Repentance is saying, "God, You are right, and I am wrong. Please forgive me."

The Bible teaches that everyone has sinned and continuation in that sin without repentance results in eternal separation from God (Romans 3:23 and 6:23). Evangelism is not a self-help program. Evangelism is the good news that when we repent of our sins, God "is faithful and just and will forgive us our sins and purify us from all unrighteousness" (1 John 1:9).

Strategic and Spontaneous

Effective evangelism in the 21st century must be intentional. It has to be planned and thought out—strategic. Jesus outlined the strategy when He told His followers, "But you will receive power when the Holy Spirit comes on you; and you will be my witnesses in Jerusalem, and in all Judea and Samaria, and to the ends of the earth" (Acts 1:8).

Many churches live out the Acts 1:8 strategy through programs that emphasize mission and ministry at the local level, state level, national level, and the international level. It's a great plan! But this strategy is as much about the individual as it is the church.

Evangelism begins in the home. From there I need to ask myself, "What can I do in my community to bring God's kingdom into reality?" "What can I do at my place of work, in my city, my state, my country, and around the world?" Jesus is not telling us to choose the one place we are most passionate about, but rather to be involved at all times at all levels. Programs are good. Programs are strategic. But ultimately, *evangelism is about living a life that proclaims Jesus every moment of every day.*

If we are truly living a life of evangelism, not only will we be strategic, we will also be spontaneous. In other words, we will look for opportunities to share the good news and take them when they come.

There are two examples in Acts of this spontaneity. First, Philip's encounter with the Ethiopian eunuch (Acts 8:26-40). Philip had been in Samaria preaching "the good news of the kingdom of God and the name of Jesus Christ" (v. 12). He had great success and many men and women believed and were baptized (v. 13). Going to Samaria was a strategic move by Philip.

Sometime later, Philip felt led by the Spirit to travel south to Gaza. While traveling, he met an Ethiopian eunuch who was reading the Bible. Philip was simply obeying God when an opportunity presented itself to share the Gospel with someone. This encounter was not strategic but spontaneous. The result, however, was the same as in Samaria. The eunuch repented, believed, and was baptized.

A second example of spontaneous evangelism is the story of Paul and Silas in prison (16:16-36). Paul delivered a slave girl from possession by a demon that had the power to predict the future. Her owners used her supernatural ability to make money for them. Once the demon left the little girl and the owners could no longer make money, they falsely accused Paul and Silas of starting a riot. As a result, the authorities threw them into prison. Being incarcerated was not part of Paul and Silas's plan; it was not a strategic move. But instead of being depressed and defeated, they worshiped and sang praises to God. While they were singing, an earthquake rattled their chains loose and opened the prison doors—not just their chains and doors, but all of the prisoners' chains and doors. The jailer, fearing reprisal from the authorities for all the escaped prisoners, was going to harm himself when, spontaneously, Paul and Silas witnessed to him. The jailer and his family repented, believed, and were baptized.

Evangelism in the 21st century will be intentional. We must plan on sharing the Gospel and strategize the most effective way to reach our communities, nation, and world. Yet while planning, we must also be open to the leading of the Holy Spirit and be willing to, at any moment, "give an answer to everyone who asks you to give the reason for the hope that you have" (1 Peter 3:15).

Emphasized Words and Actions

In Jesus Christ, God's kingdom breaks into everyday life, changing everything. Telling people of God's love and forgiveness is never enough itself. We must also show Christ in practical ways. A key trait of modernism[5] was the need for things to be rationally explained. Throughout the modern era, science was king. We now live in a postmodern[6] world and a key trait of this new mind-set is "show me." People are not as interested in how something works than if it works and what difference it makes in everyday life. While propositional statements and doctrine will always be important, practical application and doing are just as important. John the Elder put it this way, "Dear children, let us not love with words or tongue but with actions and in truth" (1 John 3:18).

The church in Acts lived out John's truth. Through faith they continued to meet people's physical needs through healing, prayer, and sacrificial giving. They were known for taking care of the poor and for truly caring for one another. Through their words and actions "the Lord added to their number daily those who were being saved" (Acts 2:47). The church in Acts cared for the whole person. Walls of discrimination based on class, gender, race, and ethnicity were broken down. Peter proclaimed, "I now realize how true it is that God does not show favoritism but accepts men from every nation who fear him and do what is right" (10:34-35). The first believers were known as much by their deeds as they were by their words.

The More Things Change

Since the birth of the church in Acts, Christianity has been on a wild journey. For two-thousand-plus years, the Gospel has been preached and lived around the world using every imaginable technique. Some methods have been more successful than others. When it comes to doing evangelism, we have been all over the map, both literally and figuratively. But the more things change, the more they remain the same.

Effective evangelism in the 21st century will adapt and use the same methods

---

5. Modernism refers to the era of Western thought that began in the 17th and 18th centuries and continued through the mid-20th century. The modern mind relied on science and technology as the major instruments of reason.

6. A single definition of what postmodern means is impossible. Rather, postmodernity refers to the deconstruction and critical thought of the modern way of reasoning.

and techniques of the first century. The believers in Acts are our example! The world they lived in was much like the world we live in—culturally and religiously diverse, secular and spiritual, immoral, lost, and far from God. I believe if we commit ourselves to Christ and pray for the kingdom of God to be present on earth as it is in heaven, we will have the same results as the first Christians. Jesus is the same yesterday, today, and forever (see Hebrews 13:8). The first Christians turned their world upside down. Through the power and presence of the Holy Spirit, we can do the same.

Keys to Chapter Three:
- "Christ" is the Greek word for "Messiah" or "Anointed One." The title "Christ," then, is a profession that Jesus is the Promised One of God prophesied in the Old Testament.
- Confessing Jesus as the "Christ" is the foundational statement of what it means to follow Jesus. It is a statement that encompasses all of who Jesus is.
- The church was born after a period of waiting on, and praying for, the Holy Spirit. The church is built through evangelism.
- Principles for evangelism for any place and any era:
    1. *Holy Spirit empowered and directed.* Apart from the presence and power of the Holy Spirit, evangelism and life change cannot take place.
    2. *Rooted in Scripture.* Evangelism is the good news that the kingdom of God has become a reality in Jesus Christ.
    3. *Centered on Jesus Christ.* The goal of evangelism is to point people to Jesus. It is in Him that God's kingdom resides.
    4. *Stressed repentance and forgiveness.* Evangelism is about Jesus and His desire and ability to forgive sins. However, sins are not forgiven until you repent. Repentance involves turning away from sin and turning to faith in Jesus.
    5. *Strategic and spontaneous.* Evangelism must be intentional and you, the evangelist, must take advantage of every opportunity that comes your way to share the good news of Jesus.
    6. *Emphasized words and actions.* Telling people of God's love and forgiveness is never enough itself. We must also show them Christ in practical ways.

- Effective evangelism in the 21st century will adapt and use the same methods and techniques of the first century.

Questions for Discussion:
1. How do you think the Holy Spirit works in evangelism? What role do you think the Holy Spirit played in your decision to follow Christ?
2. How would you explain the quote, "Effective evangelism must root itself in the teachings of Scripture, not the newest trend, the next great idea, or the most recent pop-culture, feel-good-in-the-moment motivational speech"? What do you think of that quote? Do you agree or disagree? Why?
3. Why must evangelism be centered on Jesus? What are other things the church has focused on besides Jesus?
4. What do you think it means to repent? Why do you think repentance is important to evangelism? Can a person follow Christ without repentance?
5. How would you describe the importance of both strategic and spontaneous evangelism? What is the difference? How can you be involved in both at the same time?
6. In what ways do you think actions are more important than words in evangelizing others? In what ways do you think words are more important? How do words and actions work together?

4

Evangelism and the Local Church

I worked my way through college. I had various jobs, but my favorite was as a carpenter's helper. My boss was a great guy—highly skilled and willing to teach me everything he knew. There was one problem; *I didn't want to be a carpenter.* I enjoyed the work and I learned a lot, but I didn't pay nearly as close attention as I should have because I knew that was not what I wanted to do for the rest of my life. I was a hard worker but I wasn't fully committed to being a carpenter. It was a job, not a way of life.

I remember one particular day we were remodeling a home, turning the upstairs into a separate apartment. The apartment was going to have its own entrance, which meant putting in a door where a window used to be, building a small deck, and building stairs leading to the ground. It would take fifteen steps to reach the ground. My boss excitedly tried to teach me how to determine the number of steps and the angle of the staircase. It was complicated math and I was not interested. I just wanted to help. I did not want to know how it was done.

After my sophomore year in college, I did a summer internship at a church outside of Miami, Florida. I absorbed everything I could from the host pastor like a sponge. I wanted to know how and why he did everything. I asked lots of questions. My pastor/mentor patiently answered each and every one.

A few years later, before my first pastorate, I met with a number of influential pastors, trying to gain all the wisdom I possibly could. I asked these pastors, "If I were your son and you could give me only one piece of advice before I begin my ministry, what would that advice be?" I desperately desired to learn from their experience. I was fully committed to being a minister. It wasn't a job, but a way of life.

I share these two stories in order to draw a contrast. In the first story I was nothing more than a helper. I was thankful for my job and I loved every minute of it. Well, almost every minute; there was the one occasion where my boss accidentally dropped a two-by-twelve on my head. I didn't love that moment! I used that job to get what I wanted to get out of it—namely, a paycheck.

In the second story I was more than a helper. I was an apprentice! I wanted to know and understand all the ins and outs of ministry, and I sought out mentors to help me. Twenty-plus years later, I am still trying to learn all I can. I am still seeking out more experienced ministers to mentor me. I am also mentoring others now.

If we are not careful, we fill our churches with helpers/volunteers, instead of apprentices/mentors and mentees. This happens because of a lack of understanding about the nature of biblical discipleship, and at the heart of evangelism in the local church are disciples making disciples.

Come After Me

Not long after Jesus' baptism and wilderness temptation experience, He began preaching. His message was simple, "Repent, for the kingdom of heaven is near" (Matthew 4:17).

Jesus' ministry started in Galilee, the northern province of Palestine, not far from His hometown of Nazareth. One day, as He was walking along the northern shore, He saw Peter and Andrew preparing to go fishing. Jesus said to them, "Come, follow me ... and I will make you fishers of men" (v. 19). More literally, Jesus said, "Stop what are you doing and *come after me.*" Jesus was calling Peter and Andrew to a new life of discipleship. He was calling them to be His apprentices.

In doing so, Jesus was establishing a new norm.

Traditionally, students would approach a rabbi and ask if they could be his disciple. Jesus turned that model upside down by approaching individuals and challenging them to follow Him. Traditionally, rabbis would collect a group of disciples and instruct them with the hope that one day they would instruct other pupils. Jesus turned that model inside out by calling individuals to not just learn from Him, but to live a similar life as He. Jesus' purpose was not to simply impart information. His purpose was total life change. His purpose was a deep, personal, relationship with Himself. Thus, the purpose of discipleship is not education but transformation. To follow Jesus does not mean to learn more about Him. To follow Jesus means to be His apprentice, becoming like Him, continuing His ministry of bringing God's kingdom into your reality. Jesus told His disciples, "I tell you the truth, anyone who has faith in me will do what I have been doing. *He will do even greater things than these*, because I am going to the Father"(John 14:12, emphasis mine).

Peter and Andrew were fishermen. Jesus called them to become "fishers of men" and promised He would make them such (Matthew 4:19). Throughout the Gospels, Jesus continued His comparison of adding individuals into the kingdom as fishing. He described the kingdom of heaven as "a net that was let down into the lake and caught all kinds of fish" (13:47). Not all the fish are keepers. At some point in the future, angels will "separate the wicked from the righteous and throw them into the fiery furnace" (vv. 49-50). It is our job to catch as many fish as possible. It is God's job, through the Holy Spirit, to separate and clean the fish.

Actually, our job isn't to catch the fish. Our job is to go fishing. It is Jesus' job to bring in the fish. In John 21, Jesus yelled from shore to His disciples, telling them to cast their nets on the other side of the boat. At the time, the disciples did not know it was Jesus who was yelling at them. The disciples did so and caught so many fish they were "unable to haul the net in" (v. 6).

Let's Go Fishing

As followers of Jesus, we are apprentices in the fishing business. Our "catch" is people. The "hook" God designed to bring people into the kingdom is the church. The "bait" is to continue to do what Jesus did.

What did Jesus do?

Jesus announced that the kingdom of God was near. He demonstrated what that kingdom looked like. He prayed for God's kingdom to be the same on earth as it is in heaven. He called people to repentance. He challenged people to leave everything and follow Him.

The call to evangelize is a call to do what Jesus did, and it is a very high calling. Evangelism in the local church is not a program, a Bible study, or fellowship time. Evangelism is the very DNA on which the church was born, grows, thrives, and reproduces. Evangelism in the local church comes out of discipleship, community, and intentionality. Having already discussed discipleship, we will now turn our attention to community and intentionality.

Community

Many churches include the word "community" in their name, their purpose statement, or their mission statement. The word "community" is also a buzzword in society. New neighborhoods advertise "communities" where you can walk to work, shopping, and doctor's appointments. Even businesses try to build "community" with their employees, believing that doing so will increase productivity. While there is a lot of talk about "community," few people really understand what it means and even fewer know how to live it out. Few things, however, will bring people to Christ quicker, and build their faith stronger, than real community.

What is community?

First and foremost, community is a biblical idea.

Dictionaries define "community" as social groups living in the same area or social groups who share a common interest. By that definition, a community could be a crowd, a group of acquaintances, or close friends. All dictionary definitions fall short of what the Bible means by community.

Community is part of God's DNA, as seen in the doctrine of the Trinity. A simple definition of Trinity is the belief that God is one Being equally shared in three Persons with each Person sharing the entire divine Being. Thus, God the Father is all God; God the Son is all God; and God the Holy Spirit is all God. God the Father, God the Son, and God the Holy Spirit is a divine community.

You and I were created in the image of God (Genesis 1:27). We were created to have communion with God and community with one another. However, our capacity to experience community was severely damaged when Adam and Eve sinned (chap. 3). In the beginning, Adam and Eve enjoyed uninterrupted communion with God and, as a result, enjoyed intimate communion with each other. But immediately after eating the forbidden fruit, everything changed.

When God[1] came to fellowship with Adam and Eve, they were hiding so God cried out, "Where are you?"[2] (v. 9). Adam responded, "I was afraid because I was naked; so I hid" (v. 10). God then asked, "Who told you that you were naked?" (v. 11).

It should be obvious that the idea of being naked goes beyond not wearing clothes. After God created Eve and presented her to Adam, the Bible says, "The man and his wife were both naked, and they felt no shame" (2:25). To be "naked" carries the idea of intimacy, closeness, innocence, and freedom; all of which moves us closer to the biblical idea of community. Before sin entered the world, humans enjoyed a close, personal, intimate, innocent relationship with God that also made communion with one another possible. But now, because of sin, we have been separated from God and as a result separated from one another. Written deep in our hearts, however, is a need for community; a longing to be reunited with God and one another.

God's solution to our dilemma was the death and resurrection of Jesus Christ. Through faith in Jesus we are brought back into intimate fellowship with God and, as a result, we have fellowship with one another. In other words, ***through our common unity in Christ we have community with one another.***

---

1. It is important to note that throughout the Genesis story the Hebrew word translated "God" is *Elohim*, which is plural, literally translated "Gods." This is important because it points to the Godhead (Trinity—Father, Son, Spirit) being present from eternity past and active participants in creation. For example, Genesis 1:1 reads, *"In the beginning Gods created the heavens and the earth . . ."* Since we know there is only one God, the use of *Elohim* points to the Trinity.

2. It is important to note that God took the first step in reconciling Adam and Eve to Himself. God always takes the first step. Evangelism would not be possible without God making the first move.

The preferred word in the New Testament to describe "community" is the Greek word *koinonia*, translated "fellowship," "partnership," and "communion" in various verses and translations. The basic idea behind *koinonia* is a shared participation in something that brings a deep sense of belonging. Listen to how John the Elder describes our shared participation with God, Christ, and one another:[3] *"We proclaim to you what we have seen and heard, so that you also may have **fellowship** with us. And our **fellowship** is with the Father and with his Son, Jesus Christ. . . . If we claim to have **fellowship** with him yet walk in the darkness, we lie and do not live by the truth. But if we walk in the light, as he is in the light, we have **fellowship** with one another, and the blood of Jesus, his Son, purifies us from all sin"* (1 John 1:3, 6-7).

What is the relationship between community and evangelism? Deep inside everyone's soul is a longing to belong. Intuitively we know we were created for companionship. Apart from faith in Jesus, our deepest longing goes unfulfilled. In Jesus Christ we are brought back into harmonious relationships with Him and one another. Evangelism brings people into communion and community.

When those outside the body of Christ see the body of Christ living in and living out true community, it will draw people to faith in Him. This, in part, is what Peter had in mind when he wrote, "But in your hearts set apart Christ as Lord. Always be prepared to give an answer to everyone who asks you to give the reason for the hope that you have. But do this with gentleness and respect" (1 Peter 3:15).

A wonderful example of community, and how living in community leads to evangelism, is the church in Acts 2. As followers of Jesus, they met regularly for "teaching . . . fellowship . . . breaking of bread . . . prayer" (v. 42). Of course, the word translated "fellowship" is *koinonia* and it is closely related to partaking communion (the meaning behind "breaking of bread"). Once again, community is impossible without sharing in communion with Christ.

When the believers came together, it was obvious God was with them (v. 43). The result was a unity that motivated them to share everything they had so everyone's needs were met.[4] For the church in Acts 2, community meant doing life together, sharing life. Their community was a picture of the kingdom of God that Jesus proclaimed.

Notice what happened as they lived out community: ***"And the Lord added to their number daily those who were being saved"*** (v. 47).

Community in the local church leads to evangelism in the local church. How do you build community in the local church? A very simple definition of com-

---

3. In the quote from John the Elder in 1 John, the word "fellowship" is the translation of the Greek word *koinonia*. Both the *italics* and the **bold** are for emphasis.

4. The Greek word translated "common" in Acts 2:44 is *koinos,* a form of *koinonia.*

munity is "doing life together—the good, the bad, and the ugly." Community is built by being involved in one another's lives. The New Testament uses the phrase "one another" to describe community. There are several "one another" phrases in the Bible. Chart 4.1 lists the "one another" phrases:

Chart 4.1 – "One Another" in the New Testament

"one another"	Scripture	Note or Application
accept one another	Romans 15:7–*Accept one another,* then, just as Christ accepted you, in order to bring praise to God.	One way to worship God is to accept people for who they are and who God created them to be. What hurdles do we put in people's way, making them feel unaccepted at church?
admonish one another	Colossians 3:16–*Let the word of Christ dwell in you richly as you teach and **admonish one another** with all wisdom, and as you sing psalms, hymns and spiritual songs with gratitude in your hearts to God.*	The idea behind "dwell" is to take up residence and make it your home. To "admonish" means to exhort or to instruct with the goal of life change. What do you think the relationship is between God's Word, teaching, and life change? How would you go about "admonishing" a brother or sister in Christ?
carry one another's burdens	Galatians 6:2–***Carry each other's burdens,*** *and in this way you will fulfill the law of Christ.*	In verse 5, Paul says to carry your own burdens. The idea in verse 2 is to help people who are weighted down with burdens. In context, one of the burdens that weigh people down is sin. How is the church to go about carrying one other's burdens when those burdens are a result of disobedience to God?
bear with one another	Ephesians 4:2–*Be completely humble and gentle; be patient, **bearing with one another** in love.*	To "bear with one another" means to hold each other up, enduring each other, being patient with one another, and being tolerant. The idea is to support others who are different from you and who, at times, get on your nerves. Why do you think it is important to be patient and tolerant of others in the church?
encourage one another and build one another up	1 Thessalonians 5:11–*Therefore **encourage one another** and **build each other up,** just as in fact you are doing.*	To "encourage" means to give courage to another person to keep going. Why is it so important to encourage and build up one another? In what ways do we usually discourage one another in our churches?

"one another"	Scripture	Note or Application
confess sins to one another and pray for one another	James 5:16–Therefore **confess your sins to each other** and **pray for each other** so that you may be healed. The prayer of a righteous man is powerful and effective.	In context, James relates confessing of sins and praying for each other to physical healings as well as spiritual healings. How do you think those things are connected? Is it practical to expect people to confess their sins to one another? Why or why not?
be compassionate and forgive one another	Ephesians 4:32–Be kind and **compassionate to one another, forgiving each other**, just as in Christ God forgave you.	The KJV translates "compassionate" as "tenderhearted." How can we show compassion and tenderheartedness to others? What do you think it means to forgive others in the same way God has forgiven you?
be honest with one another	Colossians 3:9–**Do not lie to each other**, since you have taken off your old self with its practices.	In what ways can we be dishonest to one another in our churches? How can we be more honest?
honor one another	Romans 12:10–**Honor one another** above yourselves.	To "honor" means to show respect and to place high value on the other person. In our churches, how can we value and respect others above ourselves?
be hospitable to one another	1 Peter 4:9–**Offer hospitality to one another** without grumbling.	In what ways can we show hospitality to one another?
love one another	Romans 13:8–Let no debt remain outstanding, except the continuing debt to **love one another.**	What do you think it means to have a "debt" of love for one another? How is this debt of love lived out in a practical way?
serve one another	Galatians 5:13–You, my brothers, were called to be free. But do not use your freedom to indulge the sinful nature; rather, **serve one another** in love.	How important is it to have an attitude of service in the church? What do you think it means to "serve one another in love"?
spur one another on	Hebrews 10:24–And let us consider how we may **spur one another on** toward love and good deeds.	The Greek phrase translated "spur one another on" means "to stimulate." The KJV translates that Greek word as "provoke." In what ways can we stimulate and provoke one another to love and good deeds?
submit to one another	Ephesians 5:21–**Submit to one another** out of reverence for Christ.	Why is it important to "submit to one another" in the church? How can we show submission to one another?

It may be idealistic, but how much more effective would your church be in evangelizing if everyone in the church lived out and lived up to the "one anothers" mentioned above? There would be no need for an "evangelism program" because the Lord would add to the church daily those who are being saved (see Acts 2:47).

Intentional

It may sound contradictory to what has already been said, but if the local church wants to evangelize, it has to make evangelism a priority and it has to have a plan in place. Think of a young married couple that wants to start a family. On the one hand, reproduction happens quite naturally. Yet on the other hand, "family planning" is vital, and being intentional about when to start a family is important.

Likewise in the church: On the one hand, a local church that is building community and making disciples will naturally evangelize. Yet on the other hand, being intentional on how to disciple, how to build community, and planning to incorporate the "one anothers" into the heart of the church is crucial to the evangelism process.

Intentionality will involve evangelism programs in the local church. It will involve training, seminars, sermons, and "how-to" demonstrations. Intentionality means taking every opportunity to talk about and stress the importance of each person sharing his faith with others. But what should be stressed is not the program, the training, the seminar, or the sermons and demonstrations. What is stressed is the fact that evangelism is about people, Jesus, and the kingdom of God.

Another huge part of being intentional about evangelism is each church committing to planting other churches. Churches starting new churches put evangelism at the very heart of the mission of the local church.

In Luke's introductory words to the Book of Acts, there is a phrase that is often overlooked. Luke writes, "In my former book, Theophilus, I wrote about all that Jesus *began* to do and to teach..." (Acts 1:1, emphasis mine)[5]. Luke is saying that Jesus "began" was to continue. How was Jesus' ministry to continue? The answer is through each local church!

Churches are organisms as well as organizations. As an organism, each local church has a lifespan of birth, growth, maturity, and death. The universal church will not die but local churches will, and that is healthy. What is not healthy are churches that do not reproduce. In the physical world, reproduction is a natural part of life. It should be no different in the spiritual world. Disciples should make disciples. Churches should plant, or help plant, other churches. The more churches there are, the more people can be added to the kingdom. Planting local churches keeps the church alive and relevant in our world. Planting local churches continues the ministry Jesus started so many years ago.

---

5. The "former book" referred to is the Gospel of Luke.

Keys to Chapter Four:
- As followers of Jesus, we are apprentices in the fishing business. Our "catch" is people. The "hook" God designed to bring people into the kingdom is the church. The "bait" is to continue to do what Jesus did.
- The call to evangelize is a call to do what Jesus did, and it is a very high calling. Evangelism is the very DNA on which the church was born, grows, thrives, and reproduces.
- Evangelism in the local church comes out of:
  - Discipleship
  - Community
  - Intentionality
- Few things bring people to Christ quicker and build their faith stronger than real community.
- Through our common unity in Christ, we have community with one another.
- When those outside the body of Christ see the body of Christ living in and living out true community, it will draw people to faith in Him.
- Community in the local church leads to evangelism in the local church.
- Chart 4.1—"One Another" in the New Testament
- On the one hand, a local church that is building community and making disciples will naturally evangelize. Yet on the other hand, being intentional on how to disciple, how to build community, and planning to incorporate the "one anothers" into the heart of the church is crucial to the evangelism process.
- Planting local churches keeps the church alive and relevant in our world.

Questions for Discussion:
1. What is the difference between a "helper" and an "apprentice"? How does knowing that difference affect how ministry is done in the local church?
2. How, and in what ways, does understanding discipleship to mean apprenticeship change your understanding of what it means to be a disciple of Jesus?

3. How would you define, describe, and illustrate community? How can community be built and maintained in the local church? What do you think is the relationship between community and evangelism?
4. Go over Chart 4.1, " 'One Another' in the New Testament," and discuss the questions asked under "Note or Application."
5. How, and in what ways, do you think your church can be more intentional about evangelism?

5

Evangelism as a Spiritual Gift

Do you know of someone who seems to have an uncanny ability to share his or her faith with perfect strangers?

Have you ever heard someone describe how he or she led someone to Christ on a short plane ride, in the elevator of an office building, or the waiting room of a doctor's office?

Have you ever been around a person who talks about his faith as easily as others talk about the weather or their favorite sports team?

Do you admire those people or do they make you feel uncomfortable... even a little guilty?

I admire them. I have known some who have made me uncomfortable. At times, some have made me feel guilty. I think all those feelings come about because deep down I wish I were more like them. There are only three problems: (1) I am an introvert by nature. (2) Evangelism is not my spiritual gift. (3) Numbers 1 and 2 are not as much problems as they are excuses.

Being an introvert is the blessing of being a middle child. I like solitude. I like silence. I like to think and read and write. The funny thing is, my calling and vocation require me to be around people all the time.[1] I don't use my introversion as an excuse not to fulfill my calling, so why do I use it as an excuse not to share my faith?

Evangelism is not my spiritual gift, but using that excuse shows my lack of understanding about both evangelism and spiritual gifts. Evangelism is unique in that the New Testament describes it not only as a spiritual gift but also as an office of the church and the personal responsibility of every believer.

---

1. I am a bi-vocational pastor. In addition to pastoring at a local church, I teach sociology classes as an adjunct professor at a local community college.

There's Something About Spiritual Gifts

The Apostle Paul knew the importance of spiritual gifts. He wrote: "Now about spiritual gifts, brothers, I do not want you to be ignorant" (1 Corinthians 12:1). The Christians in Corinth had become divided over the place and use of certain spiritual gifts in the church. By using the word "ignorant," Paul was not accusing them of being dumb or stupid; rather, he was pointing out they had erred in their understanding of spiritual gifts.

The phrase "spiritual gifts" in verse 1 is one word in the Greek, and that word is *pneumatikon,* literally meaning "spiritualities" or "spiritual things."[2] The more general word Paul uses for "spiritual gifts" (or simply "gifts," v. 4) is *charisma* or *charismata,* coming from the root *charis,* meaning "grace." Thus, a spiritual gift is a "grace-gift," a gift given to an individual by the sheer grace of God. Spiritual gifts cannot be earned; therefore, recipients of the gifts cannot brag.

What is a spiritual gift? A spiritual gift is a gift of grace given by God, through the Holy Spirit, to each believer to build God's kingdom through acts of service. To put it more simply, *spiritual gifts enable and empower the body of Christ to continue the work of Christ bringing God's kingdom into present reality.* These gifts are given, not on the basis of natural talent or worth of the individual, but according to the sovereign will of God, as He determines (see 12:11).

Natural Abilities

Spiritual gifts are not the same as natural talents. While natural talents are God-given, they have nothing to do with a person being a Christian or being a member of the body of Christ. There is no such thing as the spiritual gift of fixing automobiles, gourmet cooking, telling jokes, painting pictures, or playing basketball. However, while spiritual gifts and natural talents are different, they can be used together. For example, a person who has the spiritual gift of mercy could minister to the body of Christ by repairing a single parent's automobile, cooking for someone in need, using humor to encourage a believer going through a difficult time, painting and selling pictures and giving proceeds to missions, or using their platform of sports to tell others about the love of Christ. Everyone has natural abilities, but only believers have spiritual gifts.

Fruits of the Spirit

Spiritual gifts are not the same as the fruit of the Spirit.[3] The fruits of the Spirit build your character. The gifts of the Spirit build God's kingdom. Fruits are developed as you grow and mature in your faith. Gifts are discovered as you walk by faith. Spiritual gifts are about what you do for Christ. Spiritual fruits are

---

2. In 1 Corinthians 2:15; 3:1; and 14:37, the word is used in reference to "spiritual people." The context here (1 Corinthians 12:1ff) points to "spiritual gifts."

3. "But the fruit of the Spirit is love, joy, peace, patience, kindness, goodness, faithfulness, gentleness and self-control" (Galatians 5:22-23).

about who you are in Christ. Fruits are the result of the Holy Spirit transforming you into the image of Christ. Gifts are given by the Holy Spirit for service and ministry. Fruits are evidence you are *indwelled* by the Holy Spirit. Gifts are evidence you have been *empowered* by the Holy Spirit.

Purpose of Spiritual Gifts

In 1 Corinthians 12:2-6, Paul mentions four purposes of spiritual gifts. We will use the acronym G.I.F.T. to help us remember these purposes.

G—Grace. Spiritual gifts are a sign that God has redeemed you (12:2).

Paul doesn't want the Christians in Corinth to be "ignorant" so he reminds them from where God had brought them. He writes, "You know that when you were pagans, somehow or other you were influenced and led astray to mute idols" (12:2). Before the Corinthians became Christians, they were like prisoners being taken by armed guards to their execution—the meaning behind the phrase "led astray." Their captors were dead, useless, soundless idols. But through God's grace, Paul says, "you were washed, you were sanctified, you were justified in the name of the Lord Jesus Christ and by the Spirit of our God" (6:11).

God has given us the Holy Spirit as proof of His presence in our lives. We say when a person accepts Jesus Christ as his personal Savior, Jesus comes into his life and lives in his heart. Technically, however, it is not Jesus who indwells us, but the Holy Spirit. The Holy Spirit is the seal of our relationship with God and the source of our spiritual gifts. It is the indwelling presence of the Holy Spirit that produces fruit, but it is the empowering presence of the Holy Spirit that ministers through spiritual gifts. When you use your spiritual gifts to serve others and build up the church (evangelism), you are giving evidence that God's grace has changed you and redeemed you.

I—Identification. Spiritual gifts identify you with Jesus Christ (12:3).

Paul continues, "Therefore I tell you that no one who is speaking by the Spirit of God says, 'Jesus be cursed,' and no one can say, 'Jesus is Lord,' except by the Holy Spirit" (12:3). A person's spiritual gift identifies him with Jesus Christ and what He did on earth.

What did Christ do while on earth? He performed miracles. He healed the sick. He cast out demons. He gave life to the dead. He fed the hungry. He took in the down and out. He served the lowest of the low. He proclaimed the good news of God. He called people to repentance. He taught the truths about God. He gave people hope. In other words, He evangelized.

Then incredibly, before He left this world, He told His disciples, "I tell you the truth, anyone who has faith in me will do what I have been doing. He will do even greater things than these, because I am going to the Father" (John 14:12).

Here is an interesting question: How do we do what Jesus did, and even more than He did? By allowing the Holy Spirit to not only indwell us, but empower us for ministry through spiritual gifts! Spiritual gifts identify us with Jesus Christ.

F—Function. Spiritual gifts are given to us for service in the body of Christ (12:4-6).

First Corinthians 12:4-6 is the key to understanding spiritual gifts. Paul says, "There are different kinds of gifts, but the same Spirit. There are different kinds of service, but the same Lord. There are different kinds of working, but the same God works all of them in all men." Did you notice the reference to the Trinity in these verses? The subject of verse 5 is God the Son. The subject of verse 6 is God the Father. Each Person plays a significant role in spiritual gifts.

A key word in all three verses is the word "different." Synonyms of this Greek word[4] include "variety" and "diversity." The idea is one of "different selections." A better translation would be "distributions:" "There are *distributions* of gifts... *distributions* of service... *distributions* of working..." The word "gifts"[5] means "grace-gift; another word for "service"[6] is ministry; and the idea behind "working"[7] is "that which is accomplished."

All this leads me to believe that spiritual gifts can be categorized into three areas, with each Person of the Trinity being fundamental to each area.[8] Spiritual gifts cannot be forced into these categories, but as a tool to better understand the purpose and function of spiritual gifts, these categories can be helpful. The three categories are as follows: motivational gifts,[9] ministry gifts, and manifestation gifts.

God the Father is the key Person in distributing motivational gifts; God the Son is the key Person in distributing ministry gifts; and God the Holy Spirit is the key Person in distributing manifestation gifts. There are seven motivational gifts recorded in Romans 12:6-8; there are numerous ministry gifts, but five basic ones are recorded in Ephesians 4:11; and numerous manifestation gifts are mentioned in 1 Corinthians 12.

Here is the point: Every believer has been given a motivational gift that is to be used in ministry so God can reveal Himself through the Holy Spirit (manifestation), bringing others into the kingdom of God. Ultimately, the goal of all spiritual gifts is evangelism. Your spiritual gifts tell you how you are to function in the body of Christ.

---
4. The Greek word is *diairesis*.
5. The Greek word is *charisma*, from which we get our English word "charismatic."
6. The Greek word is *diakona*, from which we get our English word "deacon."
7. The Greek word is *energeema*, from which we get our English word "energy."
8. These suggested categories are simply for our benefit, to help our understanding, and should not be taken as anything other than that. Many of the gifts, like prophecy, could be placed in all three categories.
9. Many writers use the words "primary" or "creational" to describe what I call motivational gifts.

T—Teamwork. Spiritual gifts demonstrate unity in diversity.
Did you notice the word "same" in 1 Corinthians 12:4-6? In spite of the different distributions and variety of functions of the gifts, we are all on the same team. Unity does not mean uniformity. Unity is using our diversities to work together as a team to accomplish a common goal. We are all different, but we are all the same. Spiritual gifts are given so we can advance the kingdom of God together. Spiritual gifts show unity in the middle of diversity.

Evangelism as a Spiritual Gift

Surprisingly, there are only two places in Scripture that use the word "evangelist." In 2 Timothy 4:5, Paul admonishes Timothy to "do the work of an evangelist." An "evangelist" is a person who brings good news to people. What better news is there than in and through Jesus Christ, God's kingdom has broken into our reality? Part of the job of a pastor—and all believers—is to share their faith. Every believer has the responsibility of telling others the good news of Jesus Christ. Every believer is to "do the work of an evangelist."

In Ephesians 4:11, Paul lists five foundational office gifts given to the church by Jesus Himself. Paul writes, "It was he [Jesus] who gave some to be apostles, some to be prophets, some to be evangelists, and some to be pastors and teachers." The reason Jesus has given these gifts to the church is "to prepare God's people for works of service [evangelism being one of those services], so that the body of Christ may be built up until we all reach unity in the faith and in the knowledge of the Son of God and become mature, attaining to the whole measure of the fullness of Christ" (vv. 12-13).

From these two passages of Scripture, we see that evangelism is a spiritual gift that is given to individuals and to the church.

Evangelism as a Spiritual Gift to Individuals

As a gift given to individuals, evangelism is a ministry gift and a manifestation gift. Through the Holy Spirit, each and every believer has been given gifts to be used in ministry to continue Jesus' work on earth, bringing others into the kingdom of God. We have all been given the ability, and responsibility, to share our faith. St. Francis of Assisi[10] has been credited for saying, "Preach the gospel at all times. When necessary use words." No matter what we are doing, or what our spiritual gift may be, we are to preach Jesus. For many people, the idea of "evangelizing" is intimidating, but there is nothing to fear. The Holy Spirit has enabled, empowered, and equipped you to share your faith.

Paul discusses manifestation gifts in 1 Corinthians 12. Manifestation gifts

---
10. St. Francis (d. 1226) was a monk who lived in Assisi, Italy, and founded the Franciscan Order of monks.

are how the Holy Spirit decides to show up while you are using your spiritual gift in ministry. Manifestation gifts are the result of what you do. For example, as you use your spiritual gift of "showing mercy" (Romans 12:8), the Holy Spirit shows up and enables you to share your faith with someone and as a result, they "repent and believe" (Mark 1:15). Through your ministry gift, the manifestation gift of evangelism has been experienced.

Evangelism as a Spiritual Gift for the Church

The Apostle Paul introduces the topic of spiritual gifts in 1 Corinthians 12:1 where he writes, "Now about spiritual gifts, brothers, I do not want you to be ignorant." His main concern for the church is that they achieve unity. Unity and spiritual gifts go together. Unity is the result of everyone working together, using his or her gifts in ministry. After all, you can't rock the boat and row it at the same time. That concern for unity is also what prompts Paul to write about spiritual gifts to the church in Ephesus.

The Book of Ephesians can be divided into two sections. In chapters 1–3, Paul discusses the church's position in Christ. He writes, "Consequently, you are no longer foreigners and aliens, but fellow citizens with God's people and members of God's household.... And in him you too are being built together to become a dwelling in which God lives by his Spirit" (2:19, 22). Paul concludes this section of his letter by stating that God "is able to do immeasurably more than all we ask or imagine, according to his power that is at work within us" (3:20). That "power" at work within us is the Holy Spirit endowing us with spiritual gifts.

Chapter 4 marks the beginning of the second section in which Paul gives practical exhortations of daily Christian lifestyles. In other words, since God's Spirit lives within us, we are to live a certain way. One of the first things Paul discusses is how Christ has given the church certain *ministry* gifts.

Paul writes, "But to each one of us grace has been given as Christ apportioned it" (4:7). The word translated "grace" is *charis,* meaning "favor." *Charis* denotes the grace provided for, and manifested in, the grace-gifts. Notice, the distribution of grace—as well as grace-gifts themselves—is in Christ's own hands. They are given as He "apportioned" them. The word translated "apportioned" is where we get our English word "meter" and refers to an instrument of measurement. The New American Standard Bible translates verse 7, "But to each one of us grace was given according to the measure of Christ's gift."

In Ephesians 4:8-10, Paul gives his interpretation of Psalm 68:18. Jesus Christ left heaven and descended to earth through the incarnation. Through His death, He even descended lower (Philippians 2:5-11). But now He has ascended and sits at the right hand of God the Father (Hebrews 12:2). Before He descended in death and ascended back to heaven, He promised His disciples they would be filled with the Holy Spirit and do even greater works than He (John 14:12, 15-17). On the Day of Pentecost (Acts 2), Jesus' promise was fulfilled; the Holy Spirit came and now indwells every person who calls on the name of Jesus Christ.

How were the disciples then—and we now—to continue the work of Jesus? How is the church—the body of Christ—to carry out the ministry? We do so through the grace-gifts the Holy Spirit has given each believer and Jesus has given the church. Paul writes, "It was he [Jesus] who gave some to be apostles, some to be prophets, some to be evangelists, and some to be pastors and teachers" (Ephesians 4:11). The five ministry gifts listed here are not just gifts Christ has given individuals, but gifts He has given the church as a whole so she can continue the ministries He started. These five ministry gifts are roles people play within the body of Christ "to prepare God's people for works of service, so that the body of Christ may be built up" (v. 12). These five ministry gifts were given to the church to facilitate every member of the church to be involved in ministry through using their individual spiritual gifts.

These five gifts are offices, or roles, people play within the body of Christ to prepare others to be involved in ministry. They serve as trainers and resource people who equip the people of the church for ministry. Separate from these ministry roles in the church are numerous other ministry gifts, including but not limited to, miracles, gifts of healings, helps, leadership, spiritual language, battle, craftsmanship, exorcism, prayer, and even singleness. A person's ministry gift is what that person does within the body of Christ to build others up in their faith. A person serving in a ministry gift office serves to prepare God's people for works of service.

Literally, the word apostle (see v. 11) means "one sent forth" or "delegate." An apostle is someone sent with a message, like an ambassador of one country to another. A person with the ministry gift of apostleship has been gifted by Christ with the special ability to extend the work of the church, opening new fields to the Gospel, and overseeing larger sections of the body of Jesus Christ.

Within the church, a prophet (see v. 11) warns people of sin and calls God's people to repentance. The prophet reminds us of truths already in God's Word. A prophet can give new insight and new understanding, warn us of what may happen in the future, and, under certain conditions, tell us what will happen in the future. However, prophecy should never be equated with God's revealed will found in the Bible. All prophecy is subject to the authority of God's Word.

An evangelist (see v. 11) is one who announces the Gospel. Literally, this Greek noun translates, "tellers of a good message." The evangelist preaches Christ, keeps the message of Christ constantly before the church, and trains and encourages believers to share their faith with others. Similar to the apostles, the evangelists plant churches in areas where there are no churches. Every believer is called to share his or her faith with others. Those with this gift do so in an extraordinary way, and encourage others to do the same.

The common word in Paul's day for pastor (see v. 11) was "shepherd." Paul uses the word as a metaphor to describe those who take care of, lead, feed, and protect any local assembly of believers. Teachers (see v. 11) serve the church by making the unchanging message of God understandable. Teachers clarify truths and keep the body of Christ from errors in doctrine.

Evangelism as Personal Responsibility

Each and every disciple of Christ has the responsibility to share his or her faith with others. We are all called to continue the ministry of Jesus, proclaiming, "the kingdom of God is near. Repent and believe the good news!" (Mark 1:15). We are all called to "do the work of an evangelist" (2 Timothy 4:5). Our responsibility to share is the topic of chapter 6.

Conclusion

Evangelism is a spiritual gift, an office in the church, and the personal responsibility of every single believer. Those with the spiritual gift of evangelism have the ability to boldly share their faith and proclaim Jesus in such a way that people will listen and respond. It is a supernatural gift, not a teachable trait. A person who operates within the church as an evangelist has a way of enlisting people and training them to share their faith. The people operating in the office of an evangelist keep the focus of the church on sharing Jesus and starting new churches. When all is said and done, all of us have the privilege and responsibility to share the good news of Jesus. In Him and through Him, God's kingdom has broken into our reality, offering eternal life to all who believe.

Keys to Chapter Five:
- Evangelism is unique in that the New Testament describes it not only as a spiritual gift but also as an office of the church and the personal responsibility of every believer.
- Spiritual gifts cannot be earned; therefore, recipients of the gifts cannot brag.
- Everyone has natural abilities but only believers have spiritual gifts.
- The fruits of the Spirit build character; the gifts of the Spirit build God's kingdom.
- The purpose of spiritual gifts:

    G – Grace

    I – Identification

    F – Function

    T – Teamwork

- Every believer has been given a motivational gift that is to be used in ministry so God can reveal Himself through the Holy Spirit (manifest), bringing others into the kingdom of God.
- Evangelism is the goal of all spiritual gifts.
- The Holy Spirit has enabled, empowered, and equipped every believer to share his or her faith.

Questions for Discussion:
1. On a scale of 1 to 10 (1 being ignorant and 10 being an expert), where would you rank your knowledge of spiritual gifts? Why did you answer that way? What is your spiritual gift?
2. How would you describe the difference between spiritual gifts and natural talents?
3. How would you describe the difference between spiritual gifts and the fruits of the Spirit?
4. What are the four purposes of spiritual gifts mentioned by Paul in 1 Corinthians 12:2-6? Which one do you think is the most important? Why? In one sentence, how would you describe the purpose of spiritual gifts?
5. In what ways do you see spiritual gifts continuing the ministry of Christ in the world today? Why is this so important for evangelism?
6. Why do you think God made the "evangelist" an office in the church? What do you think the duties of the evangelist are?
7. Why do you think most believers have a hard time sharing their faith? What can be done to change that?

6

Evangelism and Personal Responsibility

I believe teaching is both my motivational and ministerial gift.[1] Through teaching, especially on college campuses, I have seen the Holy Spirit manifest Himself in incredible ways.

One evening after teaching an "Introduction to Philosophy" class, a student asked if I had time for a cup of coffee. It was already 10:00 p.m., but I could tell he really needed to talk. As we sat in a booth at a 24-hour diner sipping coffee, he told me his story.

He said he grew up in church and was baptized as a child. After high school, he attended a university but dropped out after a few semesters. By his admission he partied too hard in college and "lost" his faith after taking, of all things, a philosophy class. His philosophy professor debunked Christianity day after day. By the end of the semester, the teacher had this student convinced that Christianity and Jesus were nothing more than fables, myths, and superstition. During the following years, the student's life spiraled out of control. He was now in his late 20s with a wife, one child, and another child on the way. He realized he needed to finish his college degree. What he didn't realize was he would be taking another philosophy class, and this time the teacher would lead him back to faith in Christ.

My main subject is sociology. The school where I teach has a large international student body. Many of the students are from the Middle East; almost all of them are Muslim.

Before the start of each semester, I pray I will have a positive impact on my

---

1. See the previous chapter, "Evangelism as a Spiritual Gift" (chapter 5) for definitions and distinctions between motivational gifts, ministry gifts, and manifestation gifts.

57

students. I want to show them how a follower of Jesus acts. I don't preach, and I don't proselytize. I simply try to live out my faith. Each semester, on the very first day of class, I tell my students I am a minister. I tell them so they will know where I am coming from when they ask me a question. I make it clear that their agreeing or disagreeing with me will not affect their grades.

Not long after the end of one semester, I received an email from a student. He was a young Muslim man from Afghanistan. He asked me to write a letter of recommendation on his behalf to one of the top universities in our country. At the end of his email, this Muslim student wrote, "Dr. Riggs... I really enjoyed your class. I learned many things that actually changed the way I view people and the world. It was the only class that I looked forward to attending.... You are one of the few teachers that treated me the same no matter where I came from or what religious background I had, and I give you a lot of respect for that..."

I wrote the recommendation letter and I have never heard from this student again. My assumption is he is still Muslim.

Those two illustrations form a contrast. Our tendency is to think the first story illustrated successful evangelism while the second story did not. But I don't see it that way. I see both stories as successful evangelism stories. In both classes my prayer was the same: *may students see Jesus in me.* I believe both students did. I believe both students heard the good news that "the kingdom of God is near." I believe it was my responsibility to make sure they did. I believe evangelism is the personal responsibility of every Christ follower.

Don't Tell Anyone

After delivering His Sermon on the Mount (Matthew 5-7), as He was walking toward Capernaum, Jesus was approached by a man with leprosy who asked to be made clean (Matthew 8:1-2). Jesus healed the man and said to him, "See that you don't tell anyone" (v. 4).

Why didn't Jesus want him to tell anyone?

Jairus[2] was a well-known and prominent member of the Jewish community, a leader in the local synagogue. Jairus had one child, a daughter, nearing the age of twelve—the age a girl became a lady in ancient Jewish custom and eligible for marriage (Luke 8:41-42). These facts made her sickness all the more intense.

As Jesus was walking to Jairus's house, some people came up to them with the sad news that the young girl had died. Jesus said to Jairus, "Don't be afraid; just believe, and she will be healed" (Luke 8:50). Once in the home, Jesus went into the girl's room, took her by the hand, and said, "'*Talitha koum!*' (which means,

---

2. The story of Jesus raising Jairus's daughter from the dead is found in all three Synoptic Gospels—Matthew 9:18-26, Mark 5:21-43, and Luke 8:40-56.

'Little girl, I say to you, get up!')" (Mark 5:41). The girl got up and walked around, and then Jesus gave two commands; He asked that she be given some food, and "ordered them not to tell anyone what had happened" (Luke 8:56).

If you were healed of leprosy or had a daughter who was raised from the dead, could you keep quiet or would you want the whole world to know?

These are not the only two examples of Jesus asking for silence. On another occasion, He healed a deaf and mute man in front of a large crowd and "commanded them not to tell anyone" (Mark 7:36). He gave a blind man sight and told him, "Don't go into the village" (8:26). But maybe the most astonishing time was Peter's bold profession, after which Jesus told His disciples not to say anything to anyone.

As Jesus and His disciples were walking through the villages surrounding Caesarea Philippi, the discussion turned toward what people thought of Him. The disciples replied, "Some say John the Baptist; others say Elijah; and still others, one of the prophets" (v. 28). Jesus then asked them directly, "But what about you?... Who do you say I am?" (v. 29). Answering on behalf of the group, Peter said, "You are the Christ" (v. 29). Peter's answer was a confession of faith and a proclamation that Jesus was, and is, the anointed Son of God. After his proclamation, "Jesus warned them not to tell anyone about him" (v. 30).

You would think Jesus would want everyone to know who He was.

Not long after Peter's confession, Jesus took Peter, James, and John with Him to the top of a mountain where He was "transfigured before them.... And there appeared before them Elijah and Moses, who were talking with Jesus" (9:2, 4). Once the experience was over and they were coming down the mountain, "Jesus gave them orders not to tell anyone what they had seen" (v. 9).

Why did Jesus tell people not to tell anyone who He was or say anything about what He had done for them?

The issue seems to be one of timing. Jesus did not want to be openly proclaimed as Messiah until His formal proclamation in Jerusalem.[3] More specifically, after their experience with Jesus on the mountain with Elijah and Moses, Jesus told His disciples not to say anything "until the Son of Man had risen from the dead" (v. 9).

The irony is when Jesus told those He healed and His disciples not to tell anyone, they could not keep it quiet. Now Jesus has asked us to tell everyone about Him and we keep the good news to ourselves. Every person who professes the name of Jesus has been called, commissioned, and equipped to share the good news with others.

---
3. See Matthew 21:1-11, Mark 11:1-11, and Luke 19:28-38.

Tell Everyone

Exactly what is it we are to share?

Our message is the same as Jesus': "The time has come . . . the kingdom of God is near. Repent and believe the good news!"[4] (Mark 1:15). The Gospel is the good news that through faith in Jesus Christ, the kingdom of God becomes a present reality. In Christ, God has broken into the world to set people free and give people a new beginning.

The kingdom of God is the central message of evangelism!

After His resurrection and before His ascension, Jesus spent considerable time with His followers. His main message was the kingdom of God (Acts 1:3) and it was God's kingdom they were to share once they had received power through the Holy Spirit (v. 8).

The message of the kingdom of God found in the name of Jesus is what Philip preached (8:12).

Entrance into God's kingdom through faith in Jesus Christ was the main topic of Paul's preaching (19:8; 20:25). His last message to the Jewish leaders was about the kingdom of God. Acts reads, "They arranged to meet Paul on a certain day, and came in even larger numbers to the place where he was staying. *From morning till evening he explained and declared to them the kingdom of God and tried to convince them about Jesus . . .*" (28:23, emphasis mine). The very last words about Paul in the Book of Acts are, "Boldly and without hindrance he preached the kingdom of God and taught about the Lord Jesus Christ" (v. 31).

You can tell people a lot of information about yourself, God, the Bible, and the church. But unless you are telling them the good news that through faith in Jesus Christ, God's kingdom becomes a present reality, you have not evangelized.

Entrance into God's kingdom requires a specific response. Jesus said, "The time has come . . . the kingdom of God is near. *Repent and believe* the good news!" (Mark 1:15, emphasis mine). To repent means to change your mind and your purpose. Belief is a statement of faith—placing your complete confidence in something or Someone. Repentance and belief always go together. Repentance is a *turning away from sin,* whereas belief (or faith) is a *turning to God.*

How Do I Share My Faith?

Personal evangelism starts with how you live your life. Before people will listen to what you say, they will watch how you live. Peter writes, "But in your hearts set apart Christ as Lord. Always be prepared to give an answer to everyone who asks you to give the reason for the hope that you have. But do this with gentleness and respect" (1 Peter 3:15). People should notice hope by how we

---

4. Remember, the Greek word translated "good news" is where we get our English word "evangelism."

live our lives, and that hope should raise their curiosity so they ask us how we maintain hope in all the challenges of life. The Greek word translated "answer" is *apologia* and is the basis of our English word "apologetics." When people ask us questions based on how we have lived our lives, we are to be ready to give rational, thought-out reasons as to why we believe in Jesus.

There are three methods of sharing your faith you can practice so you will be ready when people ask: Elevator Testimony, Romans Road to Salvation, and the "Wordless Book."

Elevator Testimony

In one hundred words or less, write what your life was like before you came to Christ, what significant event led you to faith, and what difference following Jesus has made. The idea is to be able to share your story in three minutes or less; the length of an elevator ride. Sometimes, three minutes is all you have. It's a short walk across the parking lot going to and from work when a co-worker asks how you handle the stress and strain during the typical workday. It's the story you can tell as you are walking to the break room or talking to a parent in the hall during kindergarten orientation. Write your story, memorize it, and be ready to share it on a moment's notice.

Here is my example: "I grew up in church. There was never a time in my life when I did not know about Jesus. I said a lot of prayers, but nothing really changed. In seventh grade, I almost died from a football injury. God got my attention, but I still didn't get it. When I was fifteen years old, I gave my entire life to God. I asked Him to be in control. Before that time, I had no meaning and direction; but ever since that time, my life has had meaning, purpose, and direction."

If you're counting, that's ninety-two words.

Romans Road to Salvation

Sharing your story could lead to the opportunity to tell people what it means to follow Jesus. One simple way to share the Gospel story is using several verses from Romans. The first verse is Romans 3:23, "For all have sinned and fall short of the glory of God." Use this verse to emphasize that everyone has done wrong and "there is no one righteous, not even one" (v. 10).

Because we are sinful, we don't deserve the love and grace of God. Deep down most people realize this and they think they have to become good before coming to Christ. It was while we were in our sins that Jesus died for us. Romans 5:8 reads, "But God demonstrates his own love for us in this: While we were still sinners, Christ died for us."

Because of our sins we deserve death, but what God offers is life. Romans 6:23

says, "For the wages of sin is death, but the gift of God is eternal life in Christ Jesus our Lord." One result of Adam and Eve's sin (Genesis 3) is physical death that we all must endure (Romans 5:12). However, the "death" described in Romans 6:23 speaks of eternal separation from God. If we die in our sins, we will spend eternity apart from the love of God in a place the Bible calls hell. While eternal death can be earned, eternal life is given freely when we place our faith in Jesus Christ.

How do we receive eternal life? The answer is found in Romans 10:9-10, "That if you confess with your mouth, 'Jesus is Lord,' and believe in your heart that God raised him from the dead, you will be saved. For it is with your heart that you believe and are justified, and it is with your mouth that you confess and are saved."[5]

Confessing Jesus is Lord is an admission that you are not. Confessing Jesus is Lord involves confession of sin. Believing God raised Jesus from the dead is an acknowledgement that Jesus is God and through Him your sins are forgiven. Romans 10:13 adds, "Everyone who calls on the name of the Lord will be saved." To be "saved" means to be brought back into right relationship with God; to be a citizen of God's Kingdom; to have eternal life.

The "Wordless Book"

The "Wordless Book" is the Gospel story in color. Often, when working with children, people purchase different colored beads and make bracelets as they tell the story. As a young child, I learned the story of Jesus through the "Wordless Book." The colors of the book, or bracelet, are green, black, red, white, and yellow.

The color green represents creation. God created the world and everything in it, including you and me. After each day of creation (Genesis 1), God said, "It is good." God created a perfect world. But it did not stay perfect because of sin.

The color black represents sin. First, the sin of Adam and Eve (Genesis 3), but ultimately, our sins. In Romans 3:23 we are told that every person has sinned. Because God is holy, sin has to be punished and the punishment for sin is eternal separation from Him (6:23).

The color red represents the death and resurrection of Jesus. Even though we were sinners, God loved us so much He sent His Son to be the sacrifice for our sins. Jesus shed His blood so we could be forgiven. By raising Jesus from the dead, God accepted His payment for our sins.

The color white represents forgiveness of sins. When we confess our sins and through faith commit our lives to Christ, God forgives us and makes us clean. Our forgiveness is not based on what we have done, but on what Jesus did for us (10:9-10, 13).

---

5. In the next chapter, we will discuss what it means to "be saved."

The color yellow represents eternal life.[6] John 3:16 says, "For God so loved the world that he gave his one and only Son, that whoever believes in him shall not perish but have eternal life." Eternal life starts the moment you place your faith in Jesus.

There are countless ways to share your faith and tell the story of Jesus. These three are just examples. The important thing is not *how* you tell the story but *that* you tell the story.

Sharing Your Faith Without Losing Your Friends

One of the main reasons people struggle in sharing their faith is fear of offending someone. You can share your faith with "gentleness and respect" like Peter admonished. It is possible to share your faith without offending anyone. There is a story in Mark's Gospel that tells us some things we can do to make sharing our faith a positive experience for all involved.

At the end of Mark 1, Jesus heals a leper, commanding him not to tell anyone. The leper, however, could not keep quiet. As a result, "Jesus could no longer enter a town openly but stayed outside in lonely places. Yet the people still came to him from everywhere" (v. 45).

Mark continues, "A few days later, when Jesus again entered Capernaum, the people heard that he had come home. So many gathered that there was no room left, not even outside the door, and he preached the word to them" (2:1-2) Jesus returns home, and immediately people flock to Him. Jesus was preaching the kingdom of God when four industrious men brought their crippled friend to Him. Jesus healed him and forgave his sins (vv. 3-5). This brings us to the first key to sharing your faith without losing your friends.

Be completely convinced your friends need Jesus.

More than likely, the house Jesus was in was one-story with a flat roof, part of which was used as a porch and another part covered with clay, straw, and branches. Apparently, there was a stairway outside the house that went to the roof. Literally, the Bible says the men "unroofed the roof" and lowered the man down to Jesus. These men were completely convinced that the only hope for their friend was to meet Jesus.

How convinced are you that your friends need Jesus? Mark says Jesus "saw their faith" (v. 5). How is a person's faith seen? Faith is only seen when it is put into action. Can others see your faith? Are you completely convinced your friends need Jesus?

---

6. If you wanted, you could add the color blue between white and yellow and talk about the importance of baptism.

Recognize the utter helplessness of those who do not know Jesus.
The paralyzed man was completely helpless to do anything on his own. He was completely dependent on others to get him to Jesus. Likewise, in His sovereignty, God has chosen to use people to tell others about Jesus. Your friends are counting on you to get them to Jesus.

Quit making excuses.
If you were one of the four people carrying the mat, what would you have done when you got to the house and saw there was no way to get to Jesus? I probably would have said, "Well at least we tried, but it is obvious we are not going to get in."

Notice the excuses that could have been offered in this story. First, there could have been a physical excuse: "My friend is paralyzed. There is no cure for that." There could have been an excuse based on distance. We are not told how far they had to carry the man, how many steps they had to climb, or how thick the roof they had to dig through. These men did not let distance or obstacles get in their way—they just did it.

After healing the man, the story continues, "Once again Jesus went out beside the lake. A large crowd came to him, and he began to teach them. As he walked along, he saw Levi son of Alphaeus sitting at the tax collector's booth. 'Follow me,' Jesus told him, and Levi got up and followed him" (vv. 13-14).[7] Tax collectors were detested by the Jews of Jesus' day. The only thing worse than a tax collector was a Jew who was a tax collector—and that was Levi. Thus, a person's occupation could be another excuse not to bring him or her to Jesus; "I would like to tell him about Jesus, but people like that usually don't respond."

Levi responds to Jesus' call and then throws a party in His honor. The only people at the party with Jesus were other "tax collectors and sinners" (vv. 15-16). A person's lifestyle could be used as an excuse not to follow Jesus or not to tell someone about Jesus, but the greater the sin, the greater the grace. No excuse—physical, distance, criticism, crowds, occupation, lifestyle, etc.—is valid when it comes to telling your friends about Jesus.

Expect results.
If you have the best news in the world, why wouldn't your friends respond positively? The paralyzed man's sins were forgiven. Many of the "tax collectors and sinners" at Levi's party believed in Jesus. Your friend— the one you are scared to witness to—is waiting for you to tell him about Jesus. Your unchurched friend is waiting for you to invite her back into God's family.

---

7. The "lake" was the Sea of Galilee. Also, Levi is identified as Matthew in Matthew 9:9. Thus, the Levi mentioned here is Matthew, the writer of the Gospel of Matthew.

Get out of the church.
Jesus was criticized for socializing with "tax collectors and sinners." Jesus responded, "It is not the healthy who need a doctor, but the sick. I have not come to call the righteous, but sinners" (v. 17).

When I was young, my friends and I would take fishing poles with sinkers on the line and set up buckets in the backyard. We would compete with each other, seeing who could cast into the buckets. I practiced casting for hours and got pretty good. But you know what? I never caught a fish in my backyard in that bucket!

We come to church week after week, practicing being "Christian" in our little buckets. We've gotten really good at it, but we haven't caught our first fish! Why? Because the fish aren't in the bucket. The fish are outside the church walls. If we want to catch them, we have to go where they are.

Maybe you are thinking, "I know I should witness, but I just can't. I don't have the right personality." God uses all types of people and all types of personalities. Peter was confrontational; Paul was intellectual; the leper in Mark 1:45 did nothing more than testify what Jesus had done for him; the woman at the well left her water jugs and went and invited her friends to come and hear (John 4); all Levi did was invite people to his home for a meal; and in Acts 9, a lady named Dorcas witnessed by serving others, making clothes for the needy, and helping the poor. All were different, but all were effective. There is no reason you can't share your faith with others. There is every reason to share your faith.

Keys to Chapter Six:
- Evangelism is the personal responsibility of every believer.
- Every person who professes the name of Jesus has been called, commissioned, and equipped to share the good news of Jesus with others.
- The kingdom of God, in Jesus Christ, is the message of evangelism.
- Entrance into the kingdom of God requires the specific response of repentance and belief.
- Personal evangelism starts with how you live your life. Before people will listen to what you say, they will watch how you live.
- Three methods of personal evangelism:
    1. Elevator Testimony
    2. Romans Road to Salvation
    3. The "Wordless Book"

- The important thing is not *how* you tell the story but *that* you tell the story.
- Five things about sharing your faith:
    1. Be completely convinced your friends need Jesus.
    2. Recognize the utter helplessness of those who do not know Jesus.
    3. Quit making excuses.
    4. Expect results.
    5. Get out of the church.

Questions for Discussion:
1. The chapter begins with two stories. Do you think both stories are examples of evangelism? Why or why not?
2. Why do you think Jesus told people He healed not to tell anyone about Him? How difficult do you think it would have been not to tell others what Jesus had done? Could you have kept quiet?
3. Why do you think many Christians do not share their faith with others? What are some reasons why they do not?
4. How would you describe your experience with Jesus in one hundred words or less? Write out your elevator testimony and be ready to share it with your study group.
5. Of the five things you need to know about personal evangelism, which one do you think is the most important? Why? What else do you think you should know?
6. What do you think are some of the excuses people use today to not tell their friends about Jesus?

7
Evangelism and the Whole Person

People are broken. God specializes in putting broken people back together again. How did people become broken? The answer is found in the Book of Genesis. The word "genesis" means "beginnings." Thus, "In the beginning [*genesis*] God created the heavens and the earth" (Genesis 1:1).[1] These opening words of the Bible may be the most important in all of Scripture. Accept these words as truth and the rest of the Bible makes perfect sense. After this incredibly powerful opening statement, Genesis 1 outlines the seven days of creation week:

- Day 1—"And God said, 'Let there be light,' and there was light.... He separated the light from the darkness. God called the light 'day,' and the darkness he called 'night.' And there was evening, and there was morning—the first day" (Genesis 1:3-5).

- Day 2—"And God said, 'Let there be an expanse between the waters to separate water from water.' ... God called the expanse 'sky.' And there was evening, and there was morning—the second day" (vv. 6-8).

- Day 3—"And God said, 'Let the water under the sky be gathered to one place, and let dry ground appear.' ... God called the dry ground 'land,' and the gathered waters he called 'seas.'... And there was evening, and there was morning—the third day" (vv. 9-13).

- Day 4—"And God said, 'Let there be lights in the expanse of the sky to separate the day from the night, and let them serve as signs to mark

---

[1]. "Genesis" is not a Hebrew word, it is a Greek word. The first book of the Bible gets its name from the Greek translation of the Old Testament completed sometime between 300-200 B.C., called the "Septuagint." It is believed that during this time, seventy Jewish scholars were commissioned to translate the Old Testament into the Greek language. The word "Septuagint" is Latin for "seventy." Often the Septuagint is abbreviated as "LXX," the Roman numeral for seventy.

- seasons and days and years.'... And there was evening, and there was morning—the fourth day" (vv. 14, 19).
- Day 5—"And God said, 'Let the water teem with living creatures, and let birds fly above the earth across the expanse of the sky.'... And there was evening, and there was morning—the fifth day" (vv. 20, 23).
- Day 6—"And God said, 'Let the land produce living creatures according to their kinds: livestock, creatures that move along the ground, and wild animals.'... Then God said, 'Let us make man in our image, in our likeness.'... So God created man in his own image, in the image of God he created him; male and female he created them.... And there was evening, and there was morning—the sixth day" (vv. 24-31).
- Day 7—"By the seventh day God had finished the work he had been doing; so on the seventh day he rested from all his work" (2:2).

God pronounced everything He made as "very good" (1:31), meaning everything was complete, perfect, as it should be. All of creation reflects the attributes and glory of God (Psalm 19). But there is something qualitatively different about humans. You and I, and everyone else, were created in "God's image."

Created in God's Image

What does it mean to be created in the image of God? The Hebrew word translated "image" (Genesis 1:26, 27) is *tzelem,* referring to the nature and essence of a thing; an image is a representation of something else. A perfect image fully and completely represents something else. The Hebrew word translated "likeness" (v. 26) is *demut,* referring to something that is similar to something else. In no way is God saying humans were created as divine creatures or as creatures who could ascend to godlike status. Humans are not "little gods" and cannot become gods. What God is saying is humans are the highest living things in all creation, and there is something about humans that represents and reflects who He is. There is something about the very nature of humanity that is similar to the nature of God. We are images of God, without being gods ourselves, in the same way children are reflections of their parents without being their parents.

What is it about a human that is similar to the nature and essence of God? What unique traits do humans have that are not shared by other living things?

The one distinction of a human being is personhood, or personality. God is a person and man is personal. While all of creation points to a Creator, only humans are personal beings. Three things combine to make us persons: rationality, morality, and community.[2]

Rationality

Rationality refers to our ability to think, feel, and act. We think with our minds, feel with our hearts, and act with our will. Together these separate us from the rest of God's creation. All of which points to the image of God inside us.

I am an animal lover. I think I would have made a good veterinarian. I love all animals and pets, but I am partial to dogs. My Golden Retriever loves me and I love her. She has a sweet personality, and I am sure your pet does as well. I think most people understand when we ascribe our pets personalities, we don't mean the same thing as the personalities our children, friends, and spouse possess. My dog, as human as I try to make her and as much as I love her, does not reason—think, feel, and act—on the same level as people. My dog has learned that if she rolls on her back, I will scratch her tummy. She has been trained to go outside when she needs to, and is given a treat when she finishes and returns. Her instincts tell her if she wags her tail, I will pet her and speak to her in a strange, child-like voice. But she doesn't think, feel, and act like a person.

Using the ability to reason has allowed humans to accomplish and achieve incredible heights. The fact that we can explore our world, experiment with things, and create mind-blowing technologies are all evidence of us being created in God's image. New inventions and new discoveries, music and poems, great works of art and architecture—all point to the image of God in each of us. The ability of an atheist to reason there is no god and a theologian to reason the deep things of God all come from the same Source. Our desire for truth, as well as our aptitude for deceit, comes from our ability to think, feel, and act.

Rationality can be seen in the very heart of human nature in the deep questions all people ask themselves: Is there a God? If so, what does He expect of me? Is there life after death? What is the meaning and purpose of life? Why am I here? These seem to be universal, unavoidable questions, and questions only humans ask themselves and wrestle with. We ask these questions and seek answers because deep down, we know there is more to life than this life. There just has to be.

Morality

---

2. I am indebted to my college professor and advisor, F. Leroy Forlines, when it comes to understanding personhood: rationality, morality, and community (although "community" is my word, not his). I had the privilege of being his student in college and having him as my academic advisor. Much of what he taught me can be found in his book, *The Quest for Truth* (Nashville, TN: Randall House Publications, 2001), especially chapter 9, "The Nature of Man." This section is a combination of my memory of his lectures, class notes, and his various writings, and is not found in any one place.

Every semester in my "Introduction to Sociology" classes, I talk about the five elements of culture: symbols, language, norms, values, and beliefs.[3] Cultural values are the big, abstract ideas that a group of people believe to be important. Cultural beliefs are specific statements about those values. The universality of most values is amazing. All cultures value love, honesty, respect toward others, faithfulness, and family. All cultures denounce hate, lying, betrayal, and impurity. There are amazing similarities between cultures when it comes to values. The differences are in how cultures interpret those values. Cultural differences are seen in the beliefs of different cultures, not values. Thus, beauty is in the eye of the beholder; in some cultures it could be honorable to lie to your enemy; marriage is between one man and one woman, one man and more than one woman, or two people of the same sex; abortion is murder, but so is capital punishment, etc. In no way am I suggesting any type of moral equivalence when it comes to the differing beliefs among cultures. What I am suggesting is the similarities in values show that we, as humans, have a morality written on our hearts; it's part of being created in God's image. Romans 2:12-16 teaches that all persons have God's law "written on their hearts" so that everyone will be without excuse when they stand before God (Romans 1:20).

Community

A third aspect of being created in God's image is the innate desire we have to live in community. If the image of God within us refers to our personhood, that means we are personal creations who have a need to be involved in personal relationships; just like God is a personal God who desires to be involved in personal relationships.[4] Community is seen in the very nature and essence of the Godhead—Father, Son, and Spirit.

In order for us to be completely whole, we need harmony in four basic relationships: with God, with others, with ourselves, and with creation. These four relationships are either implied or expressed in Genesis 1:28-30, "God blessed [Adam and Eve] and said to them, 'Be fruitful and increase in number; fill the earth and subdue it. Rule over the fish of the sea and the birds of the air and over every living creature that moves on the ground.... I give you every seed-bearing plant on the face of the whole earth and every tree that has fruit with seed in it. They will be yours for food. And to all the beasts of the earth and all the birds of the air and all the creatures that move on the ground—everything that has the breath of life in it—I give every green plant for food.'"

---

3. Some sociologists combine "values and beliefs" into one element.

4. The idea that God is a personal God who desires a personal relationship with His creation is a uniquely Christian idea and one of the things that separates Christianity from other world religions. In most other world religions, the idea of God (or gods) being personal who wants personal relationships is blasphemy in the highest form.

First and foremost, we have a need to live in harmonious relationship with God. This desire to know God is at the very core of who we are. The reason God made humans as persons is so He could have a personal relationship with us and us with Him.

God never intended us to walk through life alone. We were created with a need to be in relationship with one another. God said, "It is not good for the man to be alone" (2:18). We are social creatures. On our own we are incomplete. We were made for community.

As human beings, we cannot make a decision or complete a task without self-examination. As a result, unlike the rest of created order, humans strive to achieve, to become better, to set goals, to climb higher, and to learn from failure. All of which deals with our relationship with ourselves.

After God created the first human, He gave him the responsibility to manage and care for the environment. The Bible says, "Then the LORD God took the man and put him in the Garden of Eden to work it and take care of it" (v. 15).[5] The psalmist wrote, "You made him [man] ruler over the works of your hands; you put everything under his feet: all flocks and herds, and the beasts of the field, the birds of the air, and the fish of the sea, all that swim the paths of the seas" (Psalm 8:6-8).

Immediately after creation, mankind was in perfect harmony with God, others, himself, and creation. Our first parents remained in perfect alignment in all four relationships for an undisclosed period of time. But then something happened that changed everything.

Brokenness and Separation

To say humans were created in the image of God and God pronounced His creation as "good," means that immediately following creation, humans had the ability to think, act, and feel in a way that was pleasing to God; and indeed they did think, act, and feel in a way that was pleasing to God. Human beings were created whole and complete, living in perfect harmony with God, others, themselves, and creation. Our first parents were about to make a bad choice. Sin was about to make an entrance, disrupting the very nature of things.

The Bible says, "Now the LORD God had planted a garden in the east, in Eden; and there he put the man he had formed. And the LORD God made all kinds of trees grow out of the ground—trees that were pleasing to the eye and good for food. In the middle of the garden were the tree of life and the tree of knowledge of good and evil" (Genesis 2:8-9).

---

5. Although no one knows for sure where the garden of Eden was, most scholars believe it was somewhere in the Middle East, quite possibly Baghdad, Iraq.

Incumbent in being created in God's image is the ability to choose. The only way God could have a personal relationship with us is to give us the choice to accept or reject Him. Before sin entered the world, humans had the capacity to choose not to sin and to live in perfect harmony with God, others, creation, and ourselves. After sin entered the world, the image of God in us was severely damaged. Before the fall,[6] our natural inclination was to choose right. Now we are born with a sinful nature, a natural bent toward choosing wrong. We are broken. The story of our brokenness, and its result, is found in Genesis 3.

At some point after creation, Eve had a conversation with a serpent.[7] We are not told what kind of serpent or how this conversation was possible. From the story, it could be inferred that the ability for a human to talk to a creature shows the harmony and wholeness mankind had with creation. In their conversation, the serpent highlighted the one thing God told our first parents not to do: eat from the tree in the middle of the garden, called the tree of the knowledge of good and evil. The consequence of eating from this tree was certain death.

Forbidden fruit always looks more appetizing than permitted fruit. The more you dwell on what is prohibited, the more open you become to lies and deceit. The serpent convincingly said to Eve, "You will not surely die.... For God knows that when you eat of it your eyes will be opened, and you will be like God, knowing good and evil" (3:4-5). Since we are created in God's image, the temptation to be "like God" is strong. Another word for that temptation is "pride" and the Bible says, "Pride goes before destruction, a haughty spirit before a fall" (Proverbs 16:18).

Convinced the fruit would be beneficial and not harmful, Eve partook and then gave some to Adam. He took a bite, and instead of dying, "the eyes of both of them were opened, and they realized they were naked; so they sewed fig leaves together and made coverings for themselves" (v. 7).

Some things are worse than death. After eating the fruit, Adam and Eve lost their innocence and their intimacy. Their capacity to think, act, and feel in a way that was pleasing to God was damaged and replaced by a self-centeredness that pushed God and others away. What died that fateful day was an intimacy with the Creator that made harmony in all other aspects of life possible. Community died and in its place was born separation.

Because of sin we are broken. We were created for relationships. When a loved one dies, the pain runs deep because we will see that person no more. There is no more fellowship, no more intimacy, and no more relationships. Death equals

---

6. "The fall" is a theological term referring to the story of the serpent and Adam and Eve. The fall of man refers to the moment they chose to eat the fruit and severely damage the image of God in which they were created. Because of the fall, we are all born with a sinful nature.

7. Notice the Bible never calls the serpent a "snake."

separation and the immediate result of sin is separation—separation from God, from each other, from ourselves, and from creation.

After Adam and Eve covered themselves they, "heard the sound of the LORD God as he was walking in the garden in the cool of the day" (v. 8). The implication seems to be that God visited them regularly. But now, when God came, they hid. God called out to them and they answered that they hid because they were naked and afraid.

God asked, "Who told you that you were naked?" (v. 11). Adam blamed Eve and Eve blamed the serpent. Neither of them wanted to take responsibility for their actions because while the fruit gave them knowledge of right and wrong, it did not give them knowledge of accountability, repentance, and reconciliation.

As a result, God cursed the serpent, cursed creation, cursed childbearing, and cursed work. God then banished Adam and Eve from the garden and from the "tree of life" (v. 22). Now, not only will they experience the death of separation, they will also experience physical death.

Because of sin, all our relationships are completely and thoroughly broken and there is nothing we can do about it. On our own, we will wander aimlessly through life without meaning, direction, and hope. On our own, we are lost.

But we are not hopeless.

Salvation and Wholeness

What we cannot do, God did!

Because of sin our natural inclination is to run away from God, but while Adam and Eve were hiding, God was calling out to them. From the very beginning it is God who initiates reconciliation with Himself. God wants to save us and put us back together again, making us whole, returning to us the ability to live in harmony with Himself, others, ourselves, and creation.

God's plan of redemption is foreshadowed in His cursing the serpent. God says, "And I will put enmity between you and the woman, and between your offspring and hers; he will crush your head, and you will strike his heel" (Genesis 3:15). This is a prophecy that is fulfilled when Jesus (God incarnated) is born of Mary and lives a righteous life but dies an awful death. Compared to what will happen to Satan (the serpent), Jesus' death will be like a heal bruise, for Jesus will total destroy (crush the head) of the enemy.

When the angel visited Joseph, instructing him to take Mary as his wife, the angel said, "She will give birth to a son, and you are to give him the name Jesus, because he will save his people from their sins" (Matthew 1:21). The name "Jesus" is the Greek version of the name "Joshua." In Hebrew, "Joshua" means, *Yahweh saves*.

The word "save" is of extreme importance. What does it mean to be "saved," especially "saved from sin"? The Greek word translated "save" is *sozo* and among other things means to heal, deliver, or restore. The idea behind *sozo* is the restoration to a former state of well-being. In other words, to be "saved" means *to be made whole again*. Because of sin, we are broken. Through faith in Jesus Christ we are made whole again. Salvation is Jesus putting us back together, restoring us to our original condition. Salvation is the process of being healed; it is the process of putting us back into right relationship with God, others, creation, and ourselves. This process will be made perfect and complete when we see Jesus face to face, but the process begins the moment we place our faith in Him.

All of Jesus' miracles had to do with Him healing broken people; making them whole again. When we repent and believe the good news, we are brought back into a right relationship with God. What was fractured in Adam and Eve is mended in Jesus. Because we are right with God, we are citizens of the kingdom where we can live in harmony with others, creation, and ourselves. Once again we have the ability to think, act, and feel in a way that is pleasing to Him.

When Jesus healed people physically, He was demonstrating what life in harmony with God and ourselves looks like. In God's kingdom, everything—including our bodies—will be perfect; there will be no more sickness, disease, disabilities, and death.

When Jesus healed people of disease, especially leprosy, He told them to go to the "priest and offer the sacrifices that Moses commanded for your cleansing, as a testimony to them" (Luke 5:14). According to the Law of Moses, a person with leprosy or other types of skin diseases could no longer live as part of the community. That person had to live outside the camp and when people approached them, they had to cry out, "Unclean! Unclean!" (Leviticus 13:45).[8] The physical disease of leprosy carried with it an emotional toll. By going before the priest and offering sacrifices, the person was announced as clean and restored to the community. The healing of leprosy involved an emotional healing as well as a physical healing.

In Mark 5:1-20, Jesus encounters a man possessed by hundreds of evil spirits. This man lived in a graveyard and could not be bound by chains. The Bible says, "Night and day among the tombs and in the hills he would cry out and cut himself with stones" (v. 5). Jesus delivered the man from his oppressors by sending the evil spirits into a herd of pigs that ran into the lake and drowned. When people came to see what had happened, "they saw the man who had been possessed by the legion of demons, *sitting there, dressed and in his right mind*" (v. 15, emphasis mine). This severely broken individual was made whole again spiritually, physically, and emotionally.

---

8. Also see Leviticus 14:1-30.

In our evangelism, if we are not careful, we will not offer people the entire Gospel. Jesus has come to put our broken lives back together again. He doesn't want to make us partially whole; He wants to make us completely whole. He wants to deliver us, heal us, and restore us back into the image of God in which we were created. This is what it means to be Christlike. Our complete restoration is a future hope, but the transformation begins the moment Jesus enters our lives. This is the good news of the Gospel! Jesus wants to bring harmony back to our lives. He wants to heal us, deliver us, and make us whole. He wants to put us back into right relationship with God, others, creation, and ourselves.

People are broken.

God specializes in putting broken people back together again.

Jesus is our great Physician.

Jesus is our great Counselor.

Jesus is our great Savior.

We have the greatest news anyone could possibly hear. Why would we not want to share it with everyone?

Keys to Chapter Seven:
- All human beings were created in the image of God.
- The one distinctive of human beings from the rest of God's creation is personhood, or personality. Three things combine to make us persons:

    1. Rationality

    2. Morality

    3. Community

- Rationality is the ability to think, feel, and act. We think with our minds, feel with our hearts, and act with our will.
- Deep down, humans know there is more to life than this life. In order to be completely whole, we need harmony in four basic relationships:

    1. with God

    2. with others

    3. with ourselves

    4. with creation (the environment)

- Incumbent in being created in God's image is the ability to choose right and wrong and to choose to accept or reject God.

- Death equals separation. The immediate result of sin is separation from God, from each other, from ourselves, and from creation.
- Salvation is Jesus putting us back together, restoring us to our original condition. This process will be made perfect and complete when we see Jesus face to face, but the process begins the moment we place our faith in Him.
- Our complete restoration is a future hope, but the transformation begins the moment Jesus enters our lives. This is the good news of the Gospel.

Questions for Discussion:
1. What do you think it means to be created in the image of God? What does it not mean?
2. How would you explain and illustrate rationality and morality to someone else? In what ways does our ability to reason and be moral distinguish us from all other aspects of God's creation?
3. In what ways do you think our need for community reflects the image of God? What do you think community means?
4. Why do you think God created us with the ability to choose? Why is this ability important for a personal relationship with God, with others, with ourselves, and with creation?
5. What do you think it means to say we are born with a sinful nature, a natural bent toward choosing wrong?

8

Evangelism and Social Justice
(Part 1)

Did you know there are over 2,100 verses in the Bible dealing with social justice? Compare that number with the following:
- There are approximately 550 Bible verses dealing with heaven.
- There are less than 100 Bible verses dealing with hell.
- There are less than 500 Bible verses deal with tithing and giving.
- If the Bible mentions something only once, it is still important as the Word of God, but considering the amount of time and space spent on social justice should show us how important the issue is to God.

How many sermons or lessons have you heard on heaven? How many books have been written about heaven? How many books have you read? What about hell? Have you heard a sermon or read a book recently about the reality of hell? What about tithing? How often do you hear the subject of money come up in a church setting?

Now compare the amount of time you have heard those topics discussed and the amount of material you have read on those subjects to the number of times you have heard of or read books on the topic of social justice. Don't get me wrong, topics like heaven, hell, and tithing are extremely important, but if God talks about justice four times as much as any of those three topics, don't you think we need to talk about it more than we do?

Social Gospel vs. Personal Conversion

Why don't more evangelical churches in the United States talk about social justice? The answer goes back to the end of 19th century and the beginning of

20th-century America. As the United States entered the Industrial Revolution, and as more and more immigrants flooded Ellis Island, churches and preachers became concerned and involved in social justice issues like caring for the poor, civil rights, unemployment, and political corruption. At the same time, more conservative churches and members became concerned with a new approach to interpreting Scripture referred to as "higher criticism."[1] This approach was raising all kinds of questions about traditionally held beliefs like the virgin birth of Christ;[2] the literal 24-hour day, seven-day creation week; and the inerrancy[3] of Scripture. Fundamentalism[4] grew out of a response to higher criticism. So, while more mainstream churches were emphasizing bringing about the kingdom of God through social justice, more conservative churches were interested in correcting doctrine and emphasizing the need for individual conversion. As a result, churches and preachers who pushed social justice issues were called "liberals" and their practices were tagged with the name "Christian Socialism"[5] and later, "Liberation Theology."[6]

Evangelicals, who came out of the conservative side of Christianity, didn't see the need to get involved in social justice issues. They were involved in compassionate ministries and did start Christian charities, but the desire and need for activism was lacking. The reason for this was because all social problems were believed to be a result of sin and the only cure for sin is personal faith in Jesus Christ, and so the emphasis should be on personal salvation not social action. Individual Christians were encouraged to get involved, but the church's mission was "evangelism" not "activism." As a result, over time the church willingly gave these issues over to the government to solve, and even then, the more liberal side of the government.

One of the results of the schism that took place among Christians in the 20th century was the battle line drawn between evangelical and mainline Christianity. Battle lines were drawn over orthodoxy and orthopraxis—right belief and right behavior. Both sides longed for cultural change, but it seemed to come down to how to best change (or at the very least, influence) culture. Mainline Christianity

---

1. Higher criticism is part of liberal theology referred to as *biblical criticism*, which took root and grew during the 1700s and 1800s. Higher criticism challenges the sources and literary methods employed by the biblical writers.
2. The doctrine of the virgin birth of Jesus states that He was miraculously conceived by Mary through the power of the Holy Spirit without any male participation.
3. Inerrancy is the belief that the Bible, as God's Word, is free from error in all its contents.
4. Fundamentalism refers to a conservative branch of theology that came about as a reaction to the liberal theology that was growing through the 1800s.
5. Christian Socialism grew out of mid-19th-century Europe as an attempt to combine the fundamental aims of socialism with the ethical teachings of Jesus and the New Testament.
6. Liberation theology emphasizes social concerns, especially the oppression of people.

took the approach that if you concentrated on changing the heart of society (Social Gospel[7]), individual hearts would change. Evangelical Christianity took the opposite approach: change the heart of the individual (personal conversion) and the heart of society would change. The Social Gospel movement lacked emphasis on personal conversion, while the emphasis on personal conversion lacked the passion to stand up against social injustices.

This schism within Christianity was clearly seen in the Civil Rights Movement. The evangelical church was slow to support civil rights as a movement.[8] In the South there was a price to pay for a white evangelical minister to get involved. Those who did were often criticized and referred to as neo-evangelicals,[9] further dividing the body of Christ. Billy Graham supported Dr. Martin Luther King, Jr., but at times, Graham's support of the movement as a whole was inconsistent, preferring revivalism and personal conversions to solve social sins over activism. This was especially true when leaders like Dr. King and others spoke out against the war in Vietnam and other social ills like poverty. The reluctance to embrace civil rights was not because evangelical churches were in favor of inequality and discrimination, but because their emphasis was on the individual and personal evangelism. Getting involved in social justice issues is not a path to salvation but it is a road those who have been saved need to travel.

Today, more and more evangelical churches are seeing the error in this thinking and are becoming more and more socially conscious. But we have a long way to go! It is time we, as evangelical Christians, take Jesus' story about sheep and goats seriously (see Matthew 25:31-46). The fundamental difference between sheep and goats is what they think and how they treat the social justice issues of their day.

What Is Social Justice?

The word "social" comes from the Latin word *socius*, meaning "companion" or "ally." The word "justice" comes from the Latin words *iustitia* and *iustus*, meaning "righteousness" and "equity." Thus, "social justice" is seeing all people as your companions or allies and treating them in a right and equitable way. Basically, "social justice" is treating others the way you want to be treated (see Matthew

---

7. "Social Gospel" is a term used to describe a movement in early 20th-century Christianity that attempted to bring social order into conformity with biblical principles. Many people consider Rev. Walter Rauschenbusch, a German Baptist pastor, to be the father of the Social-Gospel movement. Rev. Rauschenbusch worked and lived out his theology in a church in one of the poorest neighborhoods in New York City called "Hell's Kitchen." An unintended consequence of this movement is many evangelical Christians associate it with liberal theology and politics.

8. What I mean by "slow to support" refers to support from the evangelical church as a whole. There were plenty of evangelical Christians who were involved in the Civil Rights Movement from the very beginning, especially in the African American community.

9. Neo-evangelicals emphasized social responsibility.

7:12). Inherent in this definition of social justice is not simply individuals treating others rightly, but societies, communities, and governments treating others rightly. Therefore, fighting for social justice means speaking up for those who cannot speak for themselves and standing up for the rights of people who have been mistreated and oppressed. Social justice is a call, not just to individual action, but communal action as well.

The mission of the church is incomplete without being actively involved in social justice. The reason this is true is because justice is grounded in the character of God. The psalmist wrote, "Righteousness and justice are the foundation of your throne" (Psalm 89:14); and Deuteronomy 32:4 reads, "He is the Rock, his works are perfect, and all his ways are just. A faithful God who does no wrong, upright and just is he." It is for this reason that social justice has to be a part of evangelism. Evangelism, the good news that in and through Jesus, God's kingdom breaks into our reality necessitates the church's involvement in speaking out against social sins and standing up for the disenfranchised.[10]

The Voiceless Among Us

An African American pastor friend of mine, who has gone on to his reward, used to say, "If you don't constantly stir things up, the people on the bottom get burned. The prophet, Micah, put it this way, "He has showed you, O man, what is good. And what does the LORD require of you? To act justly and to love mercy and to walk humbly with your God" (Micah 6:8). God requires His people to stand up and speak out for those who cannot do so themselves. Doing so is what it means to follow Him. When we stand up for justice, we are standing up for God and His kingdom. When we stand up for justice, we should do so in merciful love and humility.

Who are those on the "bottom" of our society in danger of "getting burned"? Who are the voiceless in our society? Who are the disenfranchised? Who are the ones for whom we are to stand up and speak out?

In the Old Testament, four categories of people are continually identified as needing justice. Listen to the words of the prophet Zechariah: "This is what the LORD Almighty says: 'Administer true justice; show mercy and compassion to one another. *Do not oppress the widow or the fatherless, the alien or the poor'*" (Zechariah 7:9-10, emphasis mine). Widows, orphans, immigrants, and the poor—these are the four categories of people that have a special place in God's heart and as such, are in need of evangelism. In the days of the Old Testament prophets, these were the groups of people who had no ***social power.*** These four groups still represent a society's marginalized and disenfranchised people. To-

---
10. If you have not done so in a while, review chapters 1 and 2.

day the homeless, the elderly, single parents, and people with AIDS—just to name a few—would be added to that list. The remainder of this chapter will take a closer look at each of these groups, but first, a word about social power.

Social Power

Power is the ability to do things, to get things done, and to influence outcomes. Social power refers to who has that ability at their disposal for society as a whole. Social power is illustrated by two categories of people found in any society: the *dominant group* and the *minority group*. These two groups are not defined by numbers, but by power. The dominant group is the group that controls the power and, by controlling the power, has the advantage in society. The minority group is the group that is on the outside looking in. The minority group has no real power in the society and, as such, is disadvantaged. Dominance and minority status can be determined by gender, class, race, ethnicity, sexual orientation, educational attainment, and religion, or a combination of factors.[11] By definition, each of the four categories of people the Old Testament addresses—widows, orphans, immigrants, and the poor—are minorities with little or no power and are disadvantaged throughout all spectrums of society. If someone does not speak out and stand up for the minority group, they will be mistreated by the dominant group. Proverbs admonishes us to "speak up for those who cannot speak for themselves, for the rights of all who are destitute" (Proverbs 31:8). God commands His people to take up their cause. Doing so is a proclamation of the kingdom and is therefore a big part of evangelism.

The Widows

In the Old Testament, widows are often mentioned along with orphans. The Bible says, "For the LORD your God is God of gods and Lord of lords, the great God, mighty and awesome, who shows no partiality and accepts no bribes. He defends the cause of the fatherless and the widow..." (Deuteronomy 10:17-18). God takes seriously any mistreatment of widows and orphans. He says, "Do not take advantage of a widow or an orphan. If you do and they cry out to me, I will certainly hear their cry. My anger will be aroused, and I will kill you with the sword" (Exodus 22:22-24). This is not just an Old Testament principle. James writes, "Religion that God our Father accepts as pure and faultless is this: to look after orphans and widows in their distress..." (James 1:27).

The Hebrew word for "widows" used in the Old Testament is *almanah,* and denotes not just a woman whose husband has died but also a once-married and now divorced or abandoned woman who is in need of financial and legal

---
11. In the United States, the dominant group was founded on race, ethnicity, and religion. This dominant group is referred to by the acrostic, WASP—white, Anglo-Saxon, Protestant.

support. In ancient times, a woman's social status came through her husband or father. In the absence of those relationships, a woman had no social standing and was vulnerable to all types of abuse. The psalmist wrote that God, Himself, is "a defender of widows" (Psalm 68:5).

The need to take care of widows continued in the New Testament church. In fact, it was how to best care for widows that brought about the office of "deacon" (see Acts 6:1-7). Timothy received guidance from Paul on how to best care for widows in 1 Timothy 5:3-16. Paul admonishes Timothy to take care of "widows who are really in need." According to Paul, a "widow in need"...

- has no children or other family members who can, or will, take care of her (v. 4).
- is known as a woman of prayer (v. 5).
- does not live an exuberant lifestyle (v. 6).
- is over sixty years of age (v. 9).
- was faithful to her husband (v. 9).
- is known for her good deeds (v. 10).

If you combine widows and orphans to today's world, then you must add single parenting—especially single moms—to the list of the disenfranchised and vulnerable among us. The single largest category of people in poverty is children, followed closely by women. The situation is so dire in our country that sociologists have coined a term, "the feminization of poverty," to describe the phenomenon.

When we care for the widow, we are bringing God's kingdom into present-day reality, and if we don't, well, the Bible says, "Cursed is the man who withholds justice from . . . the widow" (Deuteronomy 27:19).

The Orphans

The Hebrew word for "orphan" is *yathom* and is often translated as "fatherless." This is why the orphan is coupled with the widow. The prophet Isaiah wrote, "Learn to do right! Seek justice, encourage the oppressed. Defend the cause of the fatherless, plead the case of the widow" (Isaiah 1:17). Any child was considered an "orphan" if he or she had no parents, or if the dad was absent—even if the child lived with his or her mom. An orphan, or fatherless child, was extremely vulnerable in society. The people of God were to care for and protect the orphan. When we do, we are bringing God's kingdom into present-day reality. The Bible says, "Cursed is the man who withholds justice from . . . the fatherless" (Deuteronomy 27:19).

The Immigrants

In the wilderness, God said to His people, "Do not mistreat an alien or oppress him, for you were aliens in Egypt" (Exodus 22:21). Another word for "alien" is "sojourner" or "foreigner." In an even stronger statement, God instructed the Israelites, "When an alien lives with you in your land, do not mistreat him. The alien living with you must be treated as one of your native-born. Love him as yourself, for you were aliens in Egypt. I am the Lord your God" (Leviticus 19:33-34). In the New Testament, Hebrews exhorts, "Do not forget to entertain strangers, for by so doing some people have entertained angels without knowing it" (Hebrews 13:2).

By definition, the immigrant is part of the minority group with very little power in society. By caring for immigrants and helping them assimilate into society, we are bringing God's kingdom into present reality. When we don't, the Bible says, "Cursed is the man who withholds justice from the alien" (Deuteronomy 27:19).

The Poor

Jesus said, "The poor you will always have with you" (Matthew 26:11), but He did not mean we should sit by and do nothing. In the context of Jesus' words, He was expressing the importance of worshiping Him, not neglecting the needy. Jesus was also quoting from Deuteronomy 15:11, "There will always be poor people in the land. Therefore I command you to be openhanded toward your brothers and toward the poor and needy in your land." The disciples would have plenty of opportunity to help the poor; helping the poor will be a continual need, but Jesus was only going to be with them a little longer.

Does God have a preference for the poor? It depends on what you mean by "preference." God does not "love" one group of people more than another. God sees sinful human nature in the rich and the poor. Both rich and poor are saved by faith in Jesus Christ. If by "preference" you mean "superiority," then no, God does not prefer the poor. However, if by "preference" you mean "priority"—not priority of importance, but "first" in a list—then yes, God does give preference to the poor. The psalmist proclaims, "Who is like you, O Lord? You rescue the poor from those too strong for them, the poor and needy from those who rob them" (Psalm 35:10); and again, "He will defend the afflicted among the people and save the children of the needy; he will crush the oppressor" (72:4).

While no one—rich or poor—should be treated unjustly, nowhere does the Bible say God defends, or rescues, the rich. The reason is because of the way social power works. The poor are disproportionately vulnerable to injustice and more likely to be victimized by those in power. The poor are easily taken advantage of by the system. What little success a poor man may have can be easily taken away. "A poor man's field may produce abundant food, but injustice sweeps it away" (Proverbs 13:23). The poor cannot stand up against the power structures of society and so they must have an advocate. God is the advocate of the poor. Jesus is the champion of the poor, and we, the body of Christ, must be the voice of the poor. When we do so, we are bringing God's kingdom into present reality.

The Least and the Last

Added to the quartet of widows, orphans, immigrants, and poor would be all those who suffer at the hands of injustice. It could be the prisoner, the leper, the prostitute, the drug addict, the sinner (including sexual sins of all orientations), the person with AIDS or some other communal disease, the mentally disabled—the list could go on. If the good news of God's kingdom is not good news to the least and the last—the widow, the orphan, the immigrant, and the poor—then it is not good news for anyone. In the words of Dr. Martin Luther King, Jr., "Injustice anywhere is a threat to justice everywhere."[12]

How Is Social Justice Related to Evangelism?

How does standing and speaking out for social justice relate to evangelism?

If evangelism is the proclamation that in and through Jesus Christ, God's kingdom is now here, then when we, through faith, become citizens of the kingdom. We also become ambassadors of His kingdom in our worlds—and that changes everything. Jesus came to redeem societies as well as individuals. As ambassadors of God's kingdom we are to model what justice and equality look like. The body of Christ (God's kingdom on earth) is to be a community that does not exclude the poor, the immigrant, the orphan, the widow, members of other races and ethnicities, or the powerless. All are welcome, and all are treated equally at the foot of the cross. This was the point of Jesus' parable about sheep and goats in Matthew 25:31-46.

Jesus tells His disciples that on the day He returns to gather all the nations before Him, He "will separate the people one from another as a shepherd separates the sheep from the goats" (v. 32). On that day, the sheep will be given a place of honor ("on his right," v. 33), while the goats will be given a place of dishonor ("on his left," v. 33). The "sheep" represent the true followers of Jesus while the "goats" represent the imposters. How will Jesus tell the difference between the sheep and the goats? What will be the distinguishing feature?

The sheep are those who continued the ministry of the Shepherd. Jesus outlined His ministry objectives in Luke 4:18-19. He said He came to give hope to the poor, freedom to the prisoner, healing to the sick, and deliverance to the

---

12. From author's notes.

oppressed. It is not too far of a stretch to see the vulnerable quartet and the least and the last in Jesus' proclamation.

In describing the ministry of the sheep, Jesus said, "For I was hungry and you gave me something to eat, I was thirsty and you gave me something to drink, I was a stranger and you invited me in, I needed clothes and you clothed me, I was sick and you looked after me, I was in prison and you came to visit me" (Matthew 25:35-36).

When the sheep (now referred to as "righteous," v. 37) asked when they did all those things, "The King will reply, 'I tell you the truth, whatever you did for one of the least of these brothers of mine, you did for me'" (v. 40).

The goats are condemned because they had done none of the things He commended the sheep for doing. The goats ignored the vulnerable ones all around them. The goats did not continue the compassionate ministry of Jesus. They did not care for the least and the last. As a result the goats were sent "away to eternal punishment, but the righteous to eternal life" (v. 46).

Throughout the New Testament you see the church continuing the ministry of caring for the poor and vulnerable. The disciples continued the healing and delivering ministry of Jesus. Church members sold what they had to meet the needs of everyone in their faith communities so that the Bible says, "There were no needy persons among them" (Acts 4:34). This is a direct reference back to God's promise in Deuteronomy when He told the Israelites that if they obeyed Him, there would be "no poor among you" (Deuteronomy 15:4). Poverty and injustice, no matter its cause or location, is a sign of God's people being disobedient to Him.

The very purpose of the office of "deacon" in the church was to take care of the physical needs of the people in the church who were the most vulnerable, especially widows. While we are to take extra care of the vulnerable within our church families, we are also obligated to stand up for the vulnerable who are not yet part of the believing community. The Apostle Paul strikes this appropriate balance by stating, "Therefore, as we have opportunity, let us do good to all people, especially to those who belong to the family of believers" (Galatians 6:10). The primary example of standing up for justice, even for those who are different from us, is Jesus' story of the Good Samaritan found in Luke 10:25-37. Jesus' main point in this story is that anyone and everyone who has a need and who has been mistreated, is our neighbor.

Caring for the poor and the needy, the vulnerable and the disenfranchised speaking out for the voiceless and standing up for the widow, the orphan, the immigrant, and the poor is a kingdom issue, and thus is an evangelism issue. Anywhere people are oppressed, mistreated, abused, and silenced, God's people must stand up for them, defend them, and minister to them. Doing so in the name of Jesus Christ brings God's kingdom into our present realm. Doing so is evangelism.

Keys to Chapter Eight:
- Social justice is seeing all people as your companions or allies and treating them in a right and equitable way. Basically, social justice is treating others the way you'd want to be treated.
- Social justice is a call, not just to individual action, but to communal action as well.
- The quartet of vulnerability in the Old Testament includes: widows, orphans, immigrants, and the poor. Added to the quartet would be the "least and the last"—the homeless, elderly, single parents, people with AIDS, etc.
- Power is the ability to do things, to get things done, and to influence outcomes. Social power refers to who has that ability at their disposal for society as a whole.
- As a matter of priorities, God gives preference to the poor because they are disproportionately vulnerable to injustice.
- If the good news of God's kingdom is not good news to the vulnerable and disenfranchised, then it is not good news for anyone.
- Jesus came to redeem societies as well as individuals.
- Poverty and injustice, no matter its cause or location, is a sign of God's people being disobedient to Him.
- Caring for the poor and the needy, the vulnerable and the disenfranchised, speaking out for the voiceless and standing up for the widow, the orphan, the immigrant, and the poor is a kingdom issue, and thus is an evangelism issue.

Questions for Discussion:
1. What do you think when you hear the term "social justice"? Why do you feel that way? Why do you think, in the past, evangelical churches struggled with getting involved in social justice issues?
2. How would you define social justice? How would you explain social justice to someone else?
3. Do you think social justice should be a part of evangelism? Why or why

not? What is the relationship between social justice and the kingdom of God?

4. Of the four categories of vulnerable people mentioned in the Old Testament, which do you think is the most vulnerable in our society today? Why did you choose that group? How should the church minister to each group?

5. What do you think it means to say God gives "preference" to the poor? What does it not mean?

6. How and in what manner will Jesus separate the sheep from the goats? What does this have to do with evangelism and social justice?

9

Evangelism and Social Justice
(Part 2)

How would you define sodomy? I'll bet your definition is drastically different from God's.

Without a doubt, the Old Testament city of Sodom was immoral and deserving of her judgment sent by God.[1] Genesis records, "Then the LORD said, 'The outcry against Sodom and Gomorrah is so great and their sin so grievous that I will go down and see if what they have done is as bad as the outcry that has reached me'" (Genesis 18:20-21).

What was Sodom's "grievous sin"?

There is an interesting story in Jewish folklore about Peletith,[2] one of Lot's daughters. According to the story, Peletith married a high-ranking official of Sodom. Every day, when Peletith would go draw water, she saw a poor man sitting by the well. She had compassion on the man and started sneaking him provisions from her house. The men of Sodom began to wonder how the poor man was surviving and when they investigated the matter, they discovered Peletith had been taking care of him. Angry at her compassion, the men had Peletith burned by fire. Before she died, Peletith prayed, "Sovereign of all the worlds, maintain my right and my cause [at the hands of] the men of Sodom." According to the story, her prayer was the outcry God heard that caused Him to act against Sodom.[3]

---

1. The story and destruction of Sodom is found in Genesis 18:16–19:29.

2. The Old Testament does not mention the names of Lot's daughters. The story of Peletith is part of Jewish tradition and folklore. There is no way to know the historical reliability of the story, but it is an interesting story nonetheless.

3. The story of Peletith is part of a collection of ancient rabbinic homilies that incorporate folklore, historical anecdotes, and moral exhortations. This particular story comes from an eighth-century midrashic teaching entitled Pirke de Rabbi Eliezer. More information can be found online at http://www.jewishencyclopedia.com/articles/12185-pirke-de-rabbi-eli-ezer.

The rest of the biblical story is full of depraved behavior by the men of Sodom. But as sinful as that depraved behavior was, it was not their most "grievous sin." The prophet Ezekiel clearly explains Sodom's sin when he said, "Now this was the sin of your sister Sodom: She and her daughters were arrogant, overfed and unconcerned; *they did not help the poor and needy.* They were haughty and did detestable things before me. *Therefore I did away with them as you have seen*" (Ezekiel 16:49-50, emphasis mine). The grievous sin of Sodom was their refusal to take care of the vulnerable and disenfranchised among them! Their grievous sin was injustice! Instead of caring for the "least of these," the people of Sodom fed their own greedy, fleshly, selfish, sexual, consumerist appetites and were judged accordingly. Sodomy, at least partially, could be defined as the absence of social justice in the community.[4] Sodomy, however it is defined, is a serious violation against the character of God.

A Quick Review

Jesus proclaimed, "'The time has come.... The kingdom of God is near. Repent and believe the good news!'" (Mark 1:15). The Greek word translated "good news" is the source of our English word "evangelism." Thus, true evangelism is announcing that in Jesus and through Jesus God's kingdom breaks into our reality.

What does the kingdom of God look like?

Jesus described it this way: "The Spirit of the Lord is on me, because he has anointed me to preach good news to the poor. He has sent me to proclaim freedom for the prisoners and recovery of sight for the blind, to release the oppressed, to proclaim the year of the Lord's favor" (Luke 4:18-19, quoting the Messianic prophecy of Isaiah 61). In God's kingdom, there will be no poverty, no crime, no imprisonment, no sickness, no oppression, and no injustice.

As a follower of Jesus, wherever I work, live, go to school, go to church, exercise, eat, vacation, or anything else, I take Jesus with me, which means God's kingdom is near. When I fight against poverty, stand against crime, minister to prisoners, heal and comfort the sick, speak up for those who are oppressed, and speak out against injustice, I am bringing God's kingdom into the here and now. I am evangelizing. Evangelism is not just getting people to say a memorized prayer (as important as that is). Evangelism is proclaiming through words and actions that God's kingdom is near. Evangelism involves both personal conversion and social consciousness: "Repent and believe the good news!"

Institutions and Issues

In the last chapter, we looked at the four categories of people the Bible men-

---
4. This is how Jewish scholars have interpreted the story of Sodom for thousands of years.

tions as the most vulnerable in any society—widows, orphans, immigrants, and the poor. We also discussed "the least and the last"—single parents, prisoners, prostitutes, drug addicts, sexual sinners, those with AIDS, etc. These people are the voiceless and the disenfranchised who live in our neighborhoods and cities, and hopefully attend our churches. Some are in their condition because of bad choices, but many more are there through bad circumstances. Regardless of the how or the why people are in the position they are in, part of evangelism is bringing the good news of the kingdom into their reality. Doing so is not easy. At times it is messy. By evangelism, I am not suggesting we simply do an "outreach" to them; rather, what I am suggesting is seeing the voiceless and disenfranchised as the very ones to whom we are called to carry the Gospel of hope. The down and out in our communities should be the church's target audience. We are to reach them, bringing them into the kingdom and our houses of worship. This is Jesus' main point in His parable of the Great Banquet in Luke 14:15-24. Jesus says, "Go out quickly into the streets and alleys of the town and bring in the poor, the crippled, the blind and the lame" (v. 21).

In this chapter, I want us to look at another quartet of social justice. This quartet is not so much individuals as it is institutions and issues that perpetuate injustices in our society. Four broad categories for discussion are *economics, equality, environment,* and *sanctity of life.*

Economics

There are basically two world economic systems: capitalism[5] and socialism.[6] Both systems have their pros and cons. Most economic systems in the world (including our own) are a combination of both. Capitalism, at least in theory, gives people the freedom to earn their own success, and there is dignity in that. Socialism, at least in theory, frees people from worrying about the basic necessities of life—food, shelter, and clothing—and there is dignity in that. The problem with socialism is that it creates apathy and diminishes ingenuity and creativity. The problem with capitalism is that it creates envy, selfishness, and greed. Neither system is perfect. Both are man-made and the heart of man is "deceitful above all things and beyond cure" (Jeremiah 17:9). There is an old Polish proverb that states, "Under capitalism man exploits man. Under socialism the reverse is true."[7]

---

5. Capitalism is an economic system in which individuals are allowed to own their own businesses or to work for others for whatever wage they can receive. The primary goal of capitalism is for people to earn their own success.

6. Socialism is an economic system in which businesses are community or government owned so there can be a more equitable distribution of goods and products. The primary goal of socialism is to insure people's basic needs of food, clothing, and shelter are met in a fair way.

7. From author's notes.

Proclaiming the kingdom of God is now here because of Jesus involves standing against economic practices that exploit people. The Bible speaks against predatory lending and unfair business practices. The Bible cautions about accumulating more and more and about building wealth on the backs of the poor. God warns employers about not paying livable wages and mistreating employees. The Bible also warns against laziness and a refusal to work. Here is just a sampling of biblical teachings:

- "He who is kind to the poor lends to the LORD, and he will reward him for what he has done" (Proverbs 19:17).
- "He who oppresses the poor to increase his wealth and he who gives gifts to the rich—both come to poverty" (Proverbs 22:16).
- "The LORD detests differing weights, and dishonest scales do not please him" (Proverbs 20:23).
- "Whoever loves wealth is never satisfied with his income" (Ecclesiastes 5:10).
- "Do not charge your brother interest, whether on money or food or anything else that may earn interest" (Deuteronomy 23:19).
- "For the love of money is a root of all kinds of evil" (1 Timothy 6:10).

Equality

Systemic inequality is all around us. It can be seen in the pay scale of women versus men, or the advantages the dominant culture has over the minority culture. It can be seen in how we treat, or mistreat, our elderly or the disabled or the homosexual. There is inequality in the classroom and the courtroom. There is even inequality in our churches. At the core of many of our societal institutions is inequality. The Bible makes it clear that people, regardless of gender, race, ethnicity, age, disabilities, class, or any other characteristic, are to be treated fairly, equitably, and as people created in the image of God. The primary Scripture dealing with equality is Jesus' own words: "So in everything, do to others what you would have them do to you" (Matthew 7:12).

Here is a sampling of some other biblical teachings about equality:

- "Then Peter began to speak: 'I now realize how true it is that God does not show favoritism but accepts men from every nation who fear him and do what is right" (Acts 10:34-35).
- "There is neither Jew nor Greek, slave nor free, male nor female, for you are all one in Christ Jesus" (Galatians 3:28).

- "Here there is no Greek or Jew, circumcised or uncircumcised, barbarian, Scythian, slave or free, but Christ is all, and is in all" (Colossians 3:11).

Environmental

I am an experienced scuba diver. I have dived in some exotic places as well as in lakes and ponds. I have seen dead fish trapped in plastic at the bottom of the ocean. I have seen corroded reefs and declining shorelines. I have also seen destruction on land. I have seen the ugly effects of mining, both in the States and in Third World countries. Parts of a small river in my hometown, a river in which I grew up swimming and fishing, have been contaminated. I believe followers of Jesus should be the first to volunteer to help restore creation. Doing so is evangelism!

At some point after creation, God placed Adam in the garden and told him to "work it and take care of it" (Genesis 2:15). God gave Adam the responsibility to "rule over the fish of the sea and the birds of the air and over every living creature that moves on the ground" (1:28). After Adam and Eve had sinned, God cursed the ground (3:17-19). But God did not relieve mankind from stewardship responsibility toward the earth. In Leviticus 25:1-7, God commands the Israelites to allow the land to rest for one year after six years of harvest so as not to overtax and overuse the natural resources the environment provides. Through the prophet Jeremiah, God suggests that one sign of people forsaking Him is their lack of care over His creation (Jeremiah 2:7).

Watching over the environment is a kingdom issue because it is our sin that has placed the planet in jeopardy. Jesus came to redeem all of God's creation, and all of God's creation longs for His return to set everything right (Romans 8:19). Protecting the environment is evangelism because God's creation points us to Him and teaches us important things about His character. The Apostle Paul writes, "For since the creation of the world God's invisible qualities—his eternal power and divine nature—have been clearly seen, being understood from what has been made, so that men are without excuse" (Romans 1:20). As we lose key elements of God's creation through extinction, destruction, overuse, and abuse, we lose knowledge of Almighty God. "Let the heavens rejoice, let the earth be glad; let the sea resound, and all that is in it; let the fields be jubilant, and everything in them. Then all the trees of the forest will sing for joy; they will sing before the LORD" (Psalm 96:11-13).

Sanctity of Life

All human life is valuable because all human life has been created in God's image. In one of his speeches to Job, Elihu confessed, "The Spirit of God has made me; the breath of the Almighty gives me life" (Job 33:4). Standing up for life most definitely means fighting for the rights of the unborn, but it could also mean speaking out against capital punishment, not because the person is innocent or because the Bible doesn't allow it under certain circumstances, but because in our society, the way capital punishment is carried out is biased against the poor who cannot afford adequate representation and applied disproportionately toward minorities. Even if one thinks the death penalty is just, the way it is carried out is ripe for abuse and injustice. We should always err on the side of life.

We need to expand sanctity of life to include fighting against human trafficking and for affordable housing. Furthermore, it should include speaking out against war, and when war is necessary, holding those responsible for war to enter war and fight war according to Just War[8] principles. Finally, included in a comprehensive sanctity of life would be understanding the need for better, more affordable, healthcare for all.

When Jesus was asked which commandment was the greatest, He replied, "'Love the Lord your God with all your heart and with all your soul and with all your mind. . . . Love your neighbor as yourself'" (Matthew 22:37-39). What better way to live out this principle than to stand up for the sanctity of all of life!

The Role of Government

Many well-meaning Christians are uncomfortable talking about the role of government in social justice, believing that God's mandate for social justice is an individual mandate, not a governmental one. Many Christians believe charity starts at home and should not be forced on us by governmental authorities. They believe the church needs to help as best it can, but leave the government out of social justice issues. I understand what they mean. I used to feel the same way. But I think this attitude comes more from a frustration with our governmental system than it does a true understanding of biblical, social justice.

The government does have a role to play, and it is a role given to it by God. I believe to properly understand the role of government, we need to differentiate between macro-social issues[9] and micro-social issues.[10]

An example of a micro issue would be a single mom living in your neighborhood who is disabled and having a hard time paying her bills. Because of a host of complex issues, she has fallen a couple of months behind on her rent and her

---

8. The Just War theory deals with the justification for fighting wars and then fighting those wars in the most humane way possible. St. Augustine and St. Thomas Aquinas, at least in part, developed the Just War theory.

9. Macro has to do with the big picture. Macro-social justice involves dealing with societal institutions that perpetuate injustice.

10. Micro has to do with the smaller picture. Micro-social justice involves caring for the disenfranchised and speaking for the voiceless as individuals and churches.

landlord is threatening eviction. Out of compassion, you and your Sunday school class collect some money and approach the church's leadership for additional help. In addition to paying her rent, you help her fill out the appropriate paperwork to start receiving disability and you help her learn how to manage her low income. You also tell her about the food closet and clothes closet at your church.

At the micro level, you volunteer to sit on a committee dealing with affordable housing, clean up a local lake or stream, march for equality on Martin Luther King Jr. Day, participate in a prayer vigil for a soon-to-be-executed convict, or a host of other issues that can—and should—be handled by individuals, churches, and organizations. There are a lot of things you can do—and should do—at the micro level.

But some social justice issues are so large they have to be addressed at the macro level. Some issues are so big they can only be rectified through governmental legislation. For example, while it was individual Christians and churches that fought to overturn slavery, only the government overturned slavery. You can fight for affordable housing, but it takes the local government to set standards and regulations on builders to build affordable houses. It takes legislation to insure disabled people have equal access to public buildings. It takes governmental involvement to pass stricter abortion laws. Since only governments can declare war, only governments can declare peace and declare a war to be unjust. At the very least, it takes governmental involvement to address the human rights issues in Uganda, the AIDS epidemic in Africa, or the human trafficking horror in our own country. We need governmental involvement at the macro level. The macro level issues are where the systemic problems lie. Furthermore, most of the Old Testament commandments about social justice issues were given to the nation of Israel, not individual Israelites.

At the micro level, I can pull people out of the rivers of poverty, a lack of education, unemployment, and hunger. But after a while, someone needs to look at the macro level issues and walk up river to see what is causing all these people to fall into the river. I think all Christians believe God will bless a nation that lives by His principles. Why then, as followers of Jesus, do we not compel our government to fight and support social justice?

Action Steps

I have a confession to make: I have not always been as concerned about the poor, the vulnerable, and the marginalized in my community. I use to be judgmental and look at people on the lower end of the socio-economic scale as lazy and uneducated. I saw the disenfranchised as people who made bad choices and who were personally responsible for their circumstances. I thought if they had been as responsible and hardworking as me, they would have never gotten themselves into their pitiful situation. Under no circumstance would I give a homeless person money because "they will just buy beer with it"; if I ever did give a person money to pay a utility bill and found out they did something else with it, something I deemed "unwise," they would never get help from me again.

God convicted me of those attitudes and over time, the Holy Spirit has transformed me into a more compassionate, more understanding person. I still have a long way to go, but I am thankful for where God has brought me and what He has taught me. I now see the system behind the people that keeps them trapped. I now see the obstacles they face in their life that I did not face. I now understand the privileged condition in which I grew up. I now see the injustice and I see the discrimination given to people of different classes and ethnicities than myself.

What changed? What opened my eyes?

First, I became friends with people different from myself. I got to know them. I sought them out. They invited me into their lives. I saw their struggles from the inside. I listened to their stories. I saw the person behind the poverty. I saw the human being behind the addiction. I saw the soul behind the marginalized. And by seeing them, I saw myself.

Second, I went on a mission trip to a Third World country. What I experienced on that first trip shook me to my knees. I saw poverty, sickness, wealth, and privilege in a new light. I try to return to that same country every year, and I take people with me. After their trip, I tell every one of them, "After seeing absolute poverty up close, if you return to the comfort of your own home and don't see the poor and marginalized in your own community, you wasted your money and time going on a mission trip."

Third, I started reading the Bible through the lens of social justice. Guess what? The Bible says more about social justice issues than it does about most other issues. Simply put, if the Gospel is not good news for the poor, then it is not good news for anyone.

Fourth, I educated myself by reading, talking and, in my case, teaching sociology. The impact of teaching sociology at a community college, where most of the students come from difficult backgrounds, had on my life cannot be overemphasized.

I try not to live with regrets but one of my main regrets is that I wasted so many years of ministry concerned about things that really are not the concern of God. In the words of Mother Teresa, "If you want to know where Jesus is, go to the poor. You will always find Him there."[11]

What can you do to embrace social justice? How can you expand your definition of evangelism to include standing up for the disenfranchised and speaking out for the voiceless? How can you change your world? Here are six action steps:

---

11. From the author's notes.

1. **Pray: Pray for God to change your heart and open your eyes to the needs around you.**
2. **Read: Read your Bible.** Read the newspaper. Read books. Educate yourself to all the needs around the world and around your community.
3. **Listen and Watch: This is part of educating yourself.** Listen to all sides of the political debate. Watch all forms of news media. Don't close your mind to people who have differing viewpoints. Open your eyes to the needs around you. Build a relationship with people different from you and listen to their stories.
4. **Pursue Your Passion: As you pray, read, and educate yourself, God will reveal a passion to you that addresses a social issue.** Pay attention to that passion.
5. **Volunteer: Volunteer at your church, but also pick out another avenue of service that addresses your passion.** It could be a local mission, a hospital, a water project, a food pantry, an environmental issue, a political issue, or cleaning up the local streams and rivers.
6. **Share: Talk to others about your passion and where you see God working.** You will be surprised how many people are waiting for someone like you to show them the way forward.

May God open our hearts and minds to the social justice issues and needs all around us. May we respond in grace, mercy, and compassion. But may we get involved.

Keys to Chapter Nine:
- The grievous sin of Sodom was the sin of injustice.
- Evangelism is proclaiming through words and actions that God's kingdom is near. Evangelism involves both personal conversion and social consciousness.
- The target audience for the church should be the down-and-out people in our communities.
- Four social justice issues and institutions: (1) Economics, (2) Equality, (3) Environment, (4) Sanctity of Life.
- Proclaiming the kingdom of God is now here because of Jesus involves standing against economic practices that exploit people.

- People, regardless of gender, race, ethnicity, age, disabilities, class, or any other characteristic, should be treated fairly, equitably, and as people created in the image of God.
- Watching over the environment is a kingdom issue because it was our sin that placed the planet in jeopardy.
- Protecting the environment is evangelism because God's creation points us to Him, teaching us important things about His character.
- We should always err on the side of life.
- Action steps for involvement in social justice: (1) Pray, (2) Read, (3) Listen and Watch, (4) Pursue Your Passion, (5) Volunteer, (6) Share.

Questions for Discussion:
1. What do you think about the sin of Sodom being injustice—not taking care of the poor and vulnerable? How does this change how you understand God's judgment on them?
2. What do you think is the relationship between evangelism and social justice?
3. What changes need to take place in your life and the life of your church to make social justice a priority?
4. How would you define economic justice?
5. Where do you see the most inequality in your life and community?
6. What role do you think justice and evangelism play in our responsibility to care for the environment?
7. In what ways do you think standing up for the sanctity of life involves more than the issue of abortion?
8. What role, if any, do you think the government should play in social justice issues?
9. Which of the six action steps listed at the end of the chapter can you apply to your life this week?

10

Evangelism in a Post-Christian World

The year was A.D. 313. In January, in the Italian city of Milan, two emperors—Constantine,[1] who ruled in the West, and Licinius,[2] who ruled in the East—met to discuss the security and welfare of the entire Roman empire. One of the topics of discussion was what to do with the Christians.

For almost three hundred years, the Romans had a love/hate relationship with this new cult.[3] Around A.D. 30, giving in to pressure from the Jewish Sanhedrin, the Roman authorities executed the Founder of this new cult, sometimes referred to as The Way. To cover his own misdeeds, Emperor Nero[4] blamed the Christians for starting a fire that destroyed a large portion of Rome. Since the cult's growth was mainly through society's lower class, many emperors left them alone, seeing them as an annoyance at worst. Other emperors fed Christians to the lions, torched them for streetlights, and persecuted them to varying degrees and effect.[5]

In spite of the persecution, Christianity continued to spread. Jesus said, "I will build my church, and the gates of Hades will not overcome it" (Matthew

---

1. Constantine was born in A.D. 272 and died in A.D. 337. He ruled as a Roman emperor in the West from A.D 306–337.

2. Licinius was born in A.D. 250 and died in A.D. 325. He ruled as a Roman emperor in the East from A.D. 308–324.

3. Early Roman authorities considered Christianity a cult because it was a new, small, monotheistic religion. Christianity was also considered a cult because it rejected emperor worship, which led to accusations that Christians were traitors.

4. Nero was born in A.D. 37 and died in A.D. 68 He was the Roman emperor from A.D. 54–68.

5. The ancient historian Tacitus (died in A.D. 117) wrote quite a bit about the persecution of Christians in first-century Rome.

16:18). At different times over the first three hundred years of Christian history, all hell had been set loose to destroy the church.

The worst of the persecution was between A.D. 303 and 311. Emperor Diocletian[6] started the harassment by issuing an edict that all churches be burned and all Scriptures destroyed. From there, things escalated to torture and martyrdom. After Diocletian stepped down, Galerius[7] continued and intensified the attacks. Some ancient writings claim that during the height of this persecution, 17,000 Christians were put to death across the empire[8] in a six-month period. Sometime around A.D. 311, Galerius became deathly ill. Reasoning that his sickness was judgment from the Christian God, Galerius changed course, ending the persecution on April 30, 311 by signing the Edict of Toleration.[9] One week later, Galerius died.

After Galerius's death, his son-in-law, Maxentius, tried to take over. This led to a showdown on October 28, 312 between Maxentius and Constantine at Milvian Bridge over the Tiber River, a few miles outside of Rome. At some point before the battle, Constantine had a vision of a Christian cross superimposed on the sun and the words, *"In hoc signo vinces,"* Latin for, "In this sign you will conquer." Convinced this was a sign from God, Constantine placed crosses on his soldiers' shields and vowed to convert to Christianity if he won the battle. Constantine was victorious. If and when he converted to Christianity has been greatly debated.

Three months later, Constantine met with Licinius and together they signed the Edict of Milan. The Edict granted religious freedom to everyone, regardless of what god or gods they worshipped. However, the Edict had tremendous effect on Christianity. By the end of the century, Christianity became the official religion of the Roman empire. In just a few hundred years, Christianity moved from a cult of the down-and-out to a religion of tremendous clout and power. The world was now "Christian."

The Modern (Christian) World

For the most part, we have lived in a Christian world since the days of Constantine, especially the West. Yes, the church has gone through struggles and schisms

---

6. Diocletian was born in A.D. 244 and died in A.D. 311. He was the Roman emperor from A.D. 284–305.

7. Galerius was born in A.D. 266 and died in A.D. 311. He was the Roman emperor from A.D. 305–311.

8. The estimate of 17,000 martyrs is found in *Liber Pontificalis* ("Book of the Popes") I.162. *Liber Pontificalis* is a biographical history of the popes, beginning with St. Peter. The first completed copy is dated around A.D. 885. There is much debate over the historical accuracy of *Liber Pontificalis* and may belong more to the genre of apocryphal literature instead of historical literature. The claim that 17,000 killed in six months seems unlikely because that would equate to approximately 95 martyrs per day. What is factual is the intensity and brutality of the persecutions during this time.

9. The Edict of Toleration allowed Christians to start meeting again. In the Edict, Galerius even asked the Christians to pray to their God on his behalf.

and has not always been stellar in her beliefs and practices, but Christianity has dominated and influenced civilization since that time.

Someone—I'm not exactly sure who—has suggested that about every five hundred years, the church holds a yard sale; out with the old and in with the new. We in the 21st century are living through another yard sale. During the first five hundred years of Christianity, Jesus lives, dies and is resurrected; the apostles take the Gospel throughout the known world and the church is born, is persecuted, and finally gets a foothold through the events of Constantine. Christianity grew from being counter-cultural to being indistinguishable from the culture.

By the end of the fifth century and into the sixth century, the Roman empire falls and the church enters a period known as the Dark Ages. During this time, there are all types of fighting and schisms. At the beginning of the eleventh century, Christianity splits into two distinct groups: Greek, or Eastern, Orthodoxy becomes the religion of the East while Roman Catholicism becomes the religion of the West.

In the West, the sixteenth century is the time of the Reformation. On October 31, 1517, Martin Luther nails his Ninety-Five Theses on the church door in Wittenberg, Germany. The result, by the 1600s, is the Protestant religion, of which our evangelical churches in the United States are a part. Now, in the 21st century (about five hundred years later), everything is changing once again.

Around the same time as the Protestant Reformation, Western civilization entered the Modern World.[10] Modernity was marked by two things: *rationalism* and *empiricism.* Rationalism is the belief that knowledge comes through reason. Rational thought is best summarized by Rene Descartes's philosophical statement, *Cogito Ergo Sum*—"I think, therefore I am."[11] Empiricism taught that rational knowledge was not enough. The only real knowledge is verifiable knowledge. In other words, you only truly know what can be experienced through the scientific method. Empirical thought is best summarized by the phrase, "Prove it to me." Western civilization remained in the modern world until the last half of the 20th century.

The Post-Christian World

One of the biggest influences modernity had on Christianity (or maybe Christianity had on modernity) was the need for and interest in *apologetics.* Faith needed to be proven and defended, and so modern Christianity moved

---

10. Most philosophers date modernity as beginning in the 1500s and ending in the mid- to late 1900s. Some will date the end of modernity as being the end of World War II.
11. Rene Descartes, a French philosopher, was born on March 31, 1596 and died on February 11, 1650.

away from "mystery"[12] to propositional statements, doctrines, and creeds. Like everything else in the modern world, Christianity needed to be rational and verifiable. But by the 1970s, Western civilization moved beyond modernity to postmodernity.[13] As a result, we no longer live in a Christian world, but a post-Christian world.

This is not bad news! To say we live in a post-Christian world is not to say that the end is near. It does not mean God is dead, Christianity is on life support, and the church is no longer relevant. What it means is "The harvest is plentiful but the workers are few" (Matthew 9:37).

Traits of the Post-Christian World

It is difficult to define the post-Christian world in one sentence or paragraph, or even in one book. One of the main reasons for this difficulty is because a trait of the post-Christian world is ***relativism.*** Relativism is a belief that all points of view are equally valid because all points of view are relative to the individual's experiences. There is no such thing as absolute truth because all truth is subject to context and culture. As a result, facts cannot be trusted because what is factual today can be falsified tomorrow. Morality is also relative and open to individual choice and interpretation.

Closely connected to relativism is the idea referred to as ***deconstruction.*** Starting in the world of literary criticism, deconstruction is a belief that no single meaning of a text is possible. Moving away from literary criticism, deconstruction involves critically evaluating why any belief is believed and why what anyone says is to be taken at face value. Deconstruction goes beyond questioning everything to questioning the possible meanings of everything. The goal of deconstruction is not to destroy meaning and belief, but to point out hidden assumptions and contradictions that affect our ability to truly understand.

A third trait of a post-Christian world is ***distrust.*** The prevailing attitude in a post-Christian world is to speak out against traditional establishments like religion. Societal institutions have been corrupted by power and can no longer be trusted. Distrust leads to a fourth trait, ***disillusionment.*** Since nothing can be trusted, nothing can be known with certainty. In a post-Christian world, people have grown weary of all the unfulfilled promises of science, technology, government, and religion.

Concerning religion, another trait of a post-Christian world is ***pluralism.*** All

---

12. The idea of "mystery" is the idea that God cannot be explained and many things about His nature need to be left to "awe." "Mystery" is extremely important to Greek, or Eastern, Orthodoxy.

13. Postmodernism is difficult to define because by its very nature it is relativistic. In a very real sense, postmodernism is whatever someone says it is.

religions are equally false and/or equally valid in that all religions offer paths to God or gods. As contradictory as it may sound, the only religions to be denounced are those that claim any type of exclusivity, especially Christianity. If Christianity is not denounced, at the very least it should be deconstructed.

A sixth trait is **environmentalism.** In a sense, protecting the environment is the religion of choice in a post-Christian world. Human societies, especially in the West, have raped and abused the earth, and so defending "Mother Earth" is of critical importance.

One last trait[14] of a post-Christian world is the significance of **globalization.** Nationalism and patriotism hinders a broader relationship with the world. All people are interconnected and all boundaries are arbitrary. Seeking the greater global good is of primary importance. On a positive note, understanding biblical environmental stewardship can be attractive to many people in a post-Christian world.

A Blessing in Disguise

Living in a post-Christian world is really a blessing in disguise. Since the days of Acts, at no time in history have people been as open to God as today. However, these same people who are open to God are closed to traditional, organized religion. Today's generation is tired of facts, figures, and a nicely put together apologetic. This does not mean apologetics is not important and a systematic theology is unnecessary. It simply means there is a different starting point in a post-Christian mind-set.

People today are looking for something real, meaningful, and lasting. In their search, they are willing to accept messy paradoxes, even contradictions. A post-Christian mind-set doesn't need everything to fit nicely together. In fact, if it fits too nicely, this generation will reject it. Now, like no time since the days of the apostles, disciples of Jesus have an opportunity to show the world the difference following Jesus makes—the good, the bad, and the ugly—without having to know all the answers.

While the modern mind-set shouted "prove it," the post-Christian mind whispers "live it." The modern mind stumbled over the miraculous and supernatural (prove the existence of God; prove the virgin birth; prove the infallibility of Scripture; prove the resurrection; etc.), while the post-Christian mind embraces—even longs for—the miraculous and supernatural. In the past, unbelievers were introduced to a good apologetic for the faith and then applied that truth to their lives. Today, many people want to know, "Does it work?" or "What dif-

---

14. The seven traits I have listed here—relativism, deconstruction, distrust, disillusionment, pluralism, environmentalism, and globalization—are more of a representative list than an exhaustive list. Several different traits could have been added.

ference will Jesus make in my life?" before they examine the deeper question of "why." Their thinking leaves the doors wide open for every believer to share his or her faith and to live his or her faith out in the public arena.

In a post-Christian world, the differences between Christian and non-Christian are more obvious, attracting the person looking for meaning and purpose in life. For years we have preached that following Jesus is about relationship, not religion. Above everything else, people in a post-Christian world are looking for real, genuine, authentic relationships.

Embracing Four Challenges

Recognizing the blessings and opportunities of living in a post-Christian world should cause us to reevaluate our approach to evangelism and embrace four challenges. The first challenge is *embracing a missional approach to evangelism*. In the past, the emphasis of evangelism was on personal conversion. While this is and will always be important and always be the goal, our churches need to understand evangelism as proclaiming the kingdom of God and all His entire kingdom entails. If we are going to take Jesus' admonition to "go into all the world" seriously, we will see that means we are to evangelize all people, all systems, all institutions, and all parts of the environment.

Our second challenge is to *be flexible in our approaches and in our expectations of evangelism*. Compromising the Gospel is not an option, but understanding we live in a different time and culture than fifty years ago is essential. A generation ago the statement, "The Bible says" was an authoritative statement. Even if people were not Christians, they knew they should be and they accepted the Bible as true. But this is no longer the case, which means we need to extend more grace and more patience when sharing Christ with others.

This leads to a third challenge and that is *using storytelling as much as propositional statements*. People are not drawn to a doctrinal treaty explaining how Christ's atonement works as much as they are drawn to a story of how belief in Jesus changed your life. Propositional statements are important, but they are important in growing in our faith, not in coming to faith.

A fourth challenge we must embrace is *allowing questions, even difficult ones, without feeling like we have to give a "correct" answer.* Often, in a post-Christian world, the permission to ask questions is more important than having those answers. In fact, if you attempt to answer all questions emphatically, you will turn the questioner away. The post-Christian mind is very comfortable with paradox and contradictions.

Advantages of Living in a Post-Christian World

The post-Christian world is a lot like the pre-Christian world and that is exciting! In the book of Acts, God took the simple message of Jesus and the ordinary people of that day who believed in Jesus and turned the world upside down. Now, in the 21st century, we have unlimited potential to once again turn our world upside down. As I see it, there are four key advantages in living in a post-Christian world:

1. *Your light becomes brighter.*

Jesus said, "You are the light of the world. A city on a hill cannot be hidden. Neither do people light a lamp and put it under a bowl. Instead they put it on its stand, and it gives light to everyone in the house. In the same way, let your light shine before men, that they may see your good deeds and glorify your Father in heaven" (Matthew 5:14-16). Light shines best in total darkness, and so the darker our society becomes, the brighter our lights will be. In a post-Christian world, the difference Jesus makes in your life will be more obvious and more attractive. As a follower of Jesus, instead of cursing the darkness, shine your light.

2. *Your hope becomes obvious.*

Because of all the despair in the world, believers have an opportune time to tell people the reason for their hope. As you live your life as a disciple of Jesus, you will have the same struggles, pressures, and stress as non-believers. However, there should be a noticeable difference in how you respond to life's challenges. Peter wrote, "But in your hearts set apart Christ as Lord. Always be prepared to give an answer to everyone who asks you to give the reason for the hope that you have. But do this with gentleness and respect" (1 Peter 3:15). Are you ready to tell people about the hope you have in Christ?

3. *Your opportunities become limitless.*

In Acts 2:41-47, Luke describes the community of the early church. They met regularly for teaching, fellowship, and prayer. As they gathered in community, they witnessed miracles and experienced powerful movements of the Holy Spirit. As a result, they sacrificially gave to one another so that everyone's needs were met. As they took advantage of all the opportunities before them, "the Lord added to their number daily those who were being saved" (v. 47). As our culture becomes more and more anti-God, the need for God will become more and more obvious. As a result, our opportunities to share the love of Christ will be limitless.

4. *Your faith becomes authentic.*

Your friends and neighbors are not looking to you to be sinless, but they are looking to you to be real and genuine. They are watching to see consistency in your life and walk with Christ. Not perfection, but authenticity. Jesus said as He is lifted up, He will draw people to Himself (John 12:32). People in a post-Christian world have an uncanny ability to spot hypocrisy. Our responsibility is to live a genuine, authentic life, one that places Jesus in the center of what we do. As we do that, He will draw people to Himself through our influence. As our world becomes darker, phony believers will disappear in the darkness. As our society becomes more intolerant toward Christians, only those who truly believe will survive, thus making faith more genuine.

Taking Advantage

We live in some incredible times. The possibilities in front of us are limitless. Now, like no other time in recent history, people are ready and waiting to hear the good news that through faith in Jesus Christ, God's kingdom becomes a present reality. The opportunities are there. Will we take advantage of them?

On one occasion, as Jesus was moving from town to town teaching, preaching, and healing, He became overwhelmed at what He saw. The needs were greater than His human potential to meet them all. Matthew describes Jesus' emotions like this: "When he saw the crowds, he had compassion on them, because they were harassed and helpless, like sheep without a shepherd. Then he said to his disciples, 'The harvest is plentiful but the workers are few. Ask the Lord of the harvest, therefore, to send out workers into his harvest field'" (Matthew 9:36-38). Some people interpret Jesus' words to be somewhat condemning. They believe Jesus is scolding His disciples—and us—because of our laziness and apathy. No doubt many believers are lazy and apathetic, but I don't believe that is Jesus' intention here. I believe He is telling His disciples—and us—that the needs are so great, and the soon-coming harvest is so large it will take all of us doing our part so as not to be overwhelmed. Instead of being overwhelmed, Jesus wants us to overcome.

How, then, do we take advantage of living in a post-Christian world?

First, we need to recognize that the time to act is now. Jesus said, "The harvest is plentiful." God has given us a wonderful opportunity to make a difference in our world, but we must act now. We need to pick the fruit before it goes bad. The best time to start evangelizing is today.

Second, we need to recognize that the work will be difficult. Jesus said, "But the workers are few." Again, the reason for so few workers is not people's unwillingness to help, but the magnitude of the coming harvest. One thing to keep in mind is the harder the work, the sweeter the reward.

A third thing that needs to be done in order to take advantage of living in a post-Christian world is to pray. Jesus continued, "Ask the Lord of the harvest." Notice that the harvest is God's, not ours. The harvest is His responsibility. Our responsibility is to obey, be diligent, and pray. If left up to us, we will be overwhelmed, but it is not up to us. It is up to God, and He is up to the task.

Finally, get involved. When Jesus said to pray that God would "send out workers into his harvest field," He was saying each of us needs to ask God what we can do and where in the field are we to work. In His sovereignty, God has decided to reach people through people. If we want to make a difference, we must get involved. That is our call. That is our challenge.

There are tremendous advantages in living in a post-Christian world, and there are plenty of opportunities before us. I pray we will take advantage of each and every one of them.

Keys to Chapter Ten:

- In the modern world, Christianity had to be rational and verifiable.

- Living in a post-Christian world does not mean God is dead, Christianity is on life-support, and the church is no longer relevant. What it means is "the harvest is plentiful but the workers are few" (Matthew 9:37).

- Traits of the post-Christian world: (1) Relativism, (2) Deconstruction, (3) Distrust, (4) Disillusionment, (5) Pluralism, (6) Environmentalism, (7) Globalization.

- Living in a post-Christian world is a blessing in disguise.

- Since the days of Acts, at no time in history have people been as open to God as today. Those same people who are open to God are closed to traditional, organized religion.

- The modern mind-set shouted, "Prove it." The post-Christian mind-set whispers, "Live it."

- Four challenges to embrace for evangelism in the 21st century:

    1. Embracing a missional approach.

    2. Being flexible in our expectations.

    3. Using storytelling as much as propositional statements.

    4. Allowing questions without feeling the need to provide "correct" answers.

- Four advantages of living in a post-Christian world:

    1. Your light becomes brighter.

    2. Your hope becomes obvious.

    3. Your opportunities become limitless.

4. Your faith becomes authentic.
- Four things we should do to take advantage of living in a post-Christian world:
  5. Recognize the time to act is now.
  6. Recognize the work will be difficult.
  7. Pray.
  8. Get involved.

Questions for Discussion:
1. How would you define rationalism and empiricism? How would you define modernity and post-modernity?
2. What do you think of the statement, "Every five hundred years, the church has a yard sale"? What do you think that statement means? How would you describe what that means to someone else?
3. What are the seven traits of a post-Christian world discussed in this chapter? Which one do you think is the most important? Why? Which trait surprises you the most? Why?
4. How, and in what ways, is living in a post-Christian world a blessing in disguise?
5. What are the challenges we need to embrace if we are to effectively evangelize in the 21st century? Which challenge do you think is the most difficult to embrace? Why? Which is the simplest? Why?
6. What do you think about the advantages of living in a post-Christian world discussed in this chapter? Do you agree or disagree with them? Why or why not?
7. What are some things you can do to take advantage of living in a post-Christian world?

11

Evangelism and the Family

People say you should never talk about religion in public. Apparently the only acceptable place to discuss religion is in private with your friends and family. I will confess, however, that I find it easier to travel to another country and share my faith with complete strangers than to talk to my friends and family about Jesus— especially my family. I don't believe I am the only person who feels this way.

Why is that?

I honestly don't know.

I am sure fear has something to do with it, as well as the risk of embarrassment and the fact our family members know us better than anyone else; they see our inconsistencies and hypocrisies. Maybe it is because we know we will not see the stranger again, but we have to live with our family.

Early in my ministry I was struggling with discouragement because my church was not growing like I thought it should. I was basing too much of my self-worth on how many people were attending each week and my self-worth was at an all-time low. My children were young at the time, and one evening while I was home, watching my kids play together and watching my wife watch the kids, God spoke to me saying, "Kevin, the most important church you will ever pastor only has four members. This church right here in your living room is where most of your attention needs to be focused." I have never forgotten those words. I will admit I have not always lived up to them, but I have never forgotten what God said. Sharing the good news of God's kingdom with your family may be difficult, but nothing worthwhile comes easy.

First Things First

Evangelizing your own family is important because we are just one generation away from not knowing anything about Jesus. God knew this and so He gave clear instructions to the Israelites to make sure they passed their faith down from one generation to the next through the family.

The central prayer among Jewish people is the *Shema*. The Hebrew word *Shema* means "to hear" and comes from the first word in the first line of the prayer: "*Hear*, O Israel: The LORD our God, the LORD is one" (Deuteronomy 6:4).[1] The entire prayer continues through Deuteronomy 6:9 and is the basic confession of the Jewish faith. The *Shema* would have been the first prayer an Israelite child memorized and then would be repeated twice a day—evening and morning[2]—as well as repeated in the synagogue. Even today, the *Shema* prayer is vital to the life of a Jewish family and community.

The entire *Shema* prayer is made up of three unifying parts.[3] Part one is the core prayer (Deuteronomy 6:4-9). The emphasis in part one is placed on the first six Hebrew words—*Shema Yisrael, Adonai eloheinu, Adonai, echad* ("Hear, O Israel: The LORD our God, the LORD is one"). When reciting, a pause would be taken after the first six words and then the rest of the prayer would be recited. The rest of the prayer stresses the importance of loving God. When asked which commandment was the greatest, Jesus quoted this part of the *Shema* prayer saying, "Love the Lord your God with all your heart and with all your soul and with all your mind" (Matthew 22:37). This fact alone should convince us of the importance of the *Shema* prayer to evangelizing the family.

The second part is recorded in Deuteronomy 11:13-21. This is the longest section of the *Shema* prayer and includes blessings for obedience and consequences for disobedience. If the Israelites are faithful "to love the LORD your God and to serve him with all your heart and with all your soul" (Deuteronomy 11:13), then God will bless them, as a nation, economically. However, a major curse of economic blessings is the temptation to turn away from God. If the people do that, "then the LORD's anger will burn against you, and he will shut the heavens so that it will not rain and the ground will yield no produce, and you will soon perish from the good land the LORD is giving you" (v. 17). The best way to avoid

---

1. *Hear* is italicized for emphasis as well as to point out that the Hebrew word being translated is *Shema*.

2. I intentionally used "evening and morning" instead of "morning and evening" because the Jewish day starts each evening and goes through the following evening. At the end of each day of Creation week (Genesis 1), God said, "And there was evening, and there was morning."

3. Each part has a specific name: Part One, Deuteronomy 6:4-9—*Shema* ("to hear"). Part Two, Deuteronomy 11:13-21—*Vehayah* ("shall come to pass"). Part Three, Numbers 15:37-41—*Vaiyomer* ("to say"). Each name reflects a significant point of the *Shema* prayer. Of course, *Shema* means we are to hear that God is One and should be loved with all our heart, soul, and mind. *Vehayah* refers to the fact that God's promises of blessing and curses, based on our obedience to Him, "shall come to pass." *Vaiyomer* reminds us that it is God who said for us to "say" to our children all the things God has done for us in the past.

that scenario is to teach your children the commands of God, the character of God, and how God has protected and provided for you (see vv. 18-21). Thus once again, you see the importance of evangelization within the family.

The final part of the *Shema* prayer is found in Numbers 15:37-41. The emphasis here is on the command to "make tassels on the corners of your garments.... You will have these tassels to look at and so you will remember all the commands of the LORD, that you may obey them" (from Numbers 15:38-39). This command is the origin of the prayer shawl still worn today by conservative Jews. In the days of Jesus, it was customary for Jewish men, especially rabbis, to wear this prayer shawl around their shoulders, hanging to the ground. When in prayer, men would lift the shawl from their shoulders and place it on their heads as a sign of humility before God, as well as to create a "secluded" place to pray. In Matthew 9:20-22, as Jesus was on His way to heal a daughter of a ruler, a woman who had been bleeding for twelve years "touched the edge of his cloak. She said to herself, 'If I only touch his cloak, I will be healed'" (Matthew 9:20-21). More than likely, what the woman touched were the "tassels" on the end of Jesus' prayer shawl. The significance of this part of the *Shema* prayer for our families is establishing customs and traditions that point our children to God and remind them of His commands.

Principles of Evangelism for the Family

Since the heart of the *Shema* prayer is Deuteronomy 6:4-9, I think it is important to take a closer look at that section in the context of the Book of Deuteronomy. These instructions are some of Moses' final words to the Israelites. Moses is now 120 years old. For forty years, he led the Israelites through the wilderness. Imagine an elderly Moses with white hair, wrinkled and sand-worn face, and a long scraggly white beard standing before the people. He knows his days are few and he leaves the Israelites with the challenge of reaching future generations for God. In his final address, there are four principles to effectively pass your faith to your children:

1. *Have a stated goal for parenting.*

While there may be accidental pregnancies, there is no such thing as an accidental birth. God has a plan for each child and He has a goal for every parent. God had two goals for the parents of Israelite children. First was to pass down their confession of faith, "Hear, O Israel: The LORD our God, the LORD is one"[4]

---

[4]. Some biblical scholars point out that the Hebrew word translated "one" is *echad* instead of *yachid*. *Yachid* is the word for the numeric "one." *Echad* carries the idea of "one" being "unified." Thus, verse 4 would read, "The Lord our God the Lord is a *unified whole."* The importance of this distinction is seeing the Trinity—Father, Son, and Spirit—in the word *echad*. A comparison verse pointed to is Genesis 2:24, "For this reason a man will leave his father and mother and be united to his wife, and they will become *one* flesh" (emphasis mine). Again, the Hebrew word translated "one" is *echad*.

(Deuteronomy 6:4). All the nations around them, including the Egyptians from whom they had recently gained freedom, were polytheistic—believing in many gods. But the God of Israel made it clear He was the one and only God. The second goal for the parents was to raise their children in the faith by keeping the Ten Commandments. In Deuteronomy 5:1-22, Moses brings the people together and reminds them of the covenant commandments of God. He introduces the Commandments by saying, "Hear [*shema*], O Israel" (v. 1).

If you are a parent, have you ever considered your purpose for being a parent? What is your goal for your children? Obtaining a good education? Becoming a good citizen? Being able to financially support himself or herself? How would you measure success as a parent? Where does God and faith in Jesus fit in the equation?

A third goal I had was to be a positive role model for them of what marriage should be. There are two aspects of this goal. First, I want my children to understand premarital sex is wrong, not because "I said so," but because marriage is a holy sacrament, and before sex is a physical and emotional act, it is a spiritual act. Waiting until marriage is worth it because marriage is worth it. I modeled this in front of my children by letting them know how much I love and adore their mother. The second aspect of this goal, which comes out of the first aspect, is modeling a God-honoring marriage in front of them. My goal is for my children to say, "When I get married, I want my marriage to be like mom and dad's marriage."

The old saying, "If you aim at nothing you are sure to hit it," applies to parenting. As a parent, you need to have the goal of evangelizing your family. Make your purpose of parenting to pass your faith and morals to your children.

2. *Build your individual relationship with God.*

You cannot lead your family to places you have not already been. If you want your family to follow God, you must follow God. The *Shema* prayer continues, "Love the LORD your God with all your heart and with all your soul and with all your strength" (Deuteronomy 6:5). Jesus said this was the greatest of all commandments (see Matthew 22:37-38), which means the greatest sin would be a violation of this commandment. Our love for God must supersede all other loves because it is only when we love God completely that we can love others correctly. This is what Jesus meant when He said, "If anyone comes to me and does not hate his father and mother, his wife and children, his brothers and sisters—yes, even his own life—he cannot be my disciple" (Luke 14:26).

The word "all" appears three times in this part of the *Shema* prayer, emphasizing the totality of our love. We are to love God with all that we have and all that we are. How total should our love be? First, we are to love God with all our "heart." The heart is the seat of our emotions. When we say we love God, we should feel something. Something inside us should be stirred. Our love for God should be alive and real, not monotonous and ritualistic.

Second, we are to love God with all our "soul." The soul is who we are; it is the part of us that is eternal. The soul is the most valuable part of you, and you are to selflessly and freely give that part of yourself to God. Nothing is more deep and meaningful than loving God with your soul.

Third, we are to love God with all our "strength." This means your love for God is strong and leads to action. Your "strength" would include your talent and your abilities, your time and your finances. One of the greatest "strengths" God has given you is your ability to reason—to think, feel, and act. When Jesus quoted the *Shema* prayer in Matthew 22:37, He was quoting the Greek translation of the Old Testament, called the *Septuagint,* and so the word "strength" was translated "mind."

To love God with all our heart, soul, and strength means we are to love Him emotionally, passionately, and rationally. We are to feel Him intimately, commit to Him eternally, and serve Him practically. If I desire my family—especially my children—to place their faith in Jesus, I must make sure my fellowship with God is what it should be. Evangelizing your family starts with evangelizing yourself.

3. *Practice what you preach.*

The *Shema* prayer continues, "These commandments that I give you today are to be upon your hearts" (Deuteronomy 6:6). Specifically, the "commandments" Moses is referring to are the Ten Commandments (5:1-21). Before God instructs the parents to pass these values down to their children, He tells them to put them "upon your hearts." In other words, your children are watching you, and your faith will be caught before it is taught.

If you don't want your children to put anything before God, you can't put anything before God (v. 7).

If you don't want your children to worship anything other than God, you can't worship anything other than God (vv. 8-10).

If you don't want your children to take God's name in vain, you can't take God's name in vain (v. 11).

If you want your children to stay in church, you must stay in church (vv. 12-15).

If you want your children to honor you, you must honor your parents (v. 16).

If you want your children to respect life, you must respect life (v. 17).

If you want your children to be faithful in their marriage, you must be faithful in your marriage (v. 18).

If you want your children to be givers instead of takers, you must be generous with what you have and not always try to get more and more (v. 19).

If you want your children to be honest in all things, you must be honest in all things (v. 20).

If you don't want your children to be envious and materialistic, you can't be envious and materialistic (v. 21).

As your children grow older, they will know you are human and make mistakes. What they are looking for is a model of how to follow God in spite of weaknesses and imperfections. Evangelizing your family hinges on you being the best example you can of what it means to follow Christ.

4. *Teach your children about God consistently.*

Moses continues, "Impress them on your children" (Deuteronomy 6:7). The Hebrew word translated "impress" is *shanan* and means "to sharpen" or even "to pierce." The idea is to teach your children about God to the point that it shapes who they are. Specifically, in the context of Deuteronomy 6, we are to impress, teach, sharpen, pierce, or shape our children's lives around the Ten Commandments, the basis of the Jewish faith and morality. By way of application, we are to impress, teach, sharpen, pierce, or shape our children's lives around all the teachings and characteristics of God.

Another basic idea behind the Hebrew word "impress" is repetition. An impression is made not by a one-time event but by continual, consistent teaching. The *Shema* prayer outlines three basic ways we are to consistently teach our children about God. First is ***informal teaching:*** "Talking about them when you sit at home and when you walk along the road, when you lie down and when you get up"(v. 7).[5] Look for every opportunity to talk about God to your children and don't let any opportunity pass. In your home, make talking about God as natural as talking about the weather, sports, or the upcoming music recital.

The second way suggested to talk about God consistently is ***formal teaching:*** "Tie them as symbols on your hands and bind them on your foreheads" (v. 8). This admonition is repeated in 11:18; "Fix these words of mine in your hearts and minds; tie them as symbols on your hands and bind them on your foreheads," and is a similar idea to the "tassels" referred to in Numbers 15:39. The early Jews took these verses literally and developed "phylacteries" (*fie-LACK-tuh-rees*) or "tefillins" (*TEE-fil-ins*), which were small pieces of paper containing the words of God that were placed in little leather boxes and tied with a band around the wrists and foreheads. These boxes were mainly worn in worship, but more pious Jews wore them throughout the day and in public. Symbolically, these things point to more formal ways to teach children through Christian education. Christian education would include taking our children to worship services and

---

5. Again, the "them" in verse 7 is specifically the Ten Commandments, but by way of application refers to all the things of God and who He is and what He has done. Also see Deuteronomy 11:19, "Teach them to your children, talking about them when you sit at home and when you walk along the road, when you lie down and when you get up."

discipleship classes, and having family devotions, etc. "Foreheads" represents our minds and "hands" represent our actions. Thus, the goal of Christian education is to get God's Word in the minds of our children so God's Word affects the actions of our children.

The third form of consistent teaching is through *family traditions:* "Write them on the doorframes of your houses and on your gates" (Deuteronomy 6:9). [6] Like the phylacteries and tefillins, the Jewish people took these words literally and would write the *Shema* prayer, especially the confession of faith, "Hear, O Israel: The LORD our God, the LORD is one" (v. 4). on the doorframes of their homes and gates to their houses. Over time, the practice became to write the entire *Shema* prayer on a piece of parchment[7] and place it in a hollowed out place on the doorframes and gates. Then, upon entering and exiting the home and gate, they would place their right hand on the door and gate and say the prayer.

Evangelism in the family doesn't just happen. You have to be intentional about it. When it comes to passing your faith down to your children, you have a window of opportunity that closes quickly. There are no guarantees, but you will never be sorry for teaching, or impressing, your children about the things of God.

A Family Portrait

A Christian family is a picture of life in the kingdom of God. When members of the family live out their faith by fulfilling their role in the family, that family itself becomes an evangelism tool pointing others to faith in Jesus Christ. What does that type of family look like? What are the roles of family members?

The Apostle Paul reveals the roles of wives, husbands, children, and parents in Colossians, chapter 3. First, to the wives he explains, "Wives, submit to your husbands, as is fitting in the Lord" (Colossians 3:18). The basis for this admonition is functional. A better translation of the Greek word translated "submit" (*hupotassesthe*) is "yield." The meaning is that in the operation of the home, the wife should voluntarily "yield" to the decisions of the husband as long as his decisions do not violate the character and words of God. It is important to note that the issue of yielding or submissiveness is not superiority and inferiority—the issue isn't even the relationship between men and women in general; rather, the issue is the relationship between husband and wife.

To the husbands, Paul writes, "Husbands, love your wives and do not be harsh with them" (v. 19). *Agape,* the Greek word translated "love," is the highest form of

---

6. Also see Deuteronomy 11:20, "Write them on the doorframes of your houses and on your gates, so that your days and the days of your children may be many in the land that the LORD swore to give your forefathers, as many as the days that the heavens are above the earth."

7. A "parchment" is a thin piece of leather, usually sheep or goatskin, that was used as paper in ancient days.

love possible. *Agape* love is the type of unconditional love God has for us. It is a love that is sacrificial. It is a love that treats your wife with kindness and respect, and as someone to be valued. These words by Paul were revolutionary. In his day, wives were possessions of their husbands with no legal standing or rights. In God's kingdom, there is no distinction between male and female except in the roles of husbands and wives. In reality, if a husband loves his wife the way God commands, the issue of yielding would no longer be an issue.

In reference to children, Paul continues, "Children, obey your parents in everything, for this pleases the Lord" (v. 20). Obedience is vital to the health and well-being of a child. Children who do not learn to obey parents will struggle with authority in other areas of life. Obeying parents is how children learn to obey all authority, including how they learn to obey God.

The word translated "fathers" in verse 21 was a term sometimes used for both parents: "Fathers, do not embitter your children, or they will become discouraged." This warning is to parents to make sure they discipline their children, but not in such a way as to kill their spirits. However, it should be noted that while the word "fathers" could include both parents, the primary responsibility for leadership and discipline in the home lies on the shoulders of dad, not mom.

What If?

Ideally, the home is a picture of God's kingdom, and evangelism in the home evangelizes the community. But not all homes are ideal; in fact, very few homes are ideal. In many homes only one parent follows God. What do you do if you are the only spouse in the family committed to Christ? Believe it or not, the Bible addresses this issue.

In the seventh chapter of Paul's first letter to the Christians in Corinth, he goes into some detail about marriage.[8] Beginning in verse 12, he addresses believers who have unbelieving spouses. Paul's advice to both husbands and wives was that as long as the non-believing spouse agrees to stay in the marriage relationship, they should stay. By staying with the unbelieving spouse, the believing spouse brings blessings and honor into the home. However, if the unbelieving spouse abandons the family, then divorce is permissible if reconciliation is not possible because "God has called us to live in peace" (v. 15).

The Apostle Peter addresses the same concern in 1 Peter 3:1-6. His words are to women with unbelieving husbands, but the applications would work both ways. Peter's advice is for the believing spouse to let his or her actions "win over" the unbelieving spouse. In the home, actions speak louder than words, and good behavior works far better than nagging among spouses.

The home is the foundation of all society. It does little good to talk about

---
8. See 1 Corinthians 7:12-17.

evangelizing the world without first evangelizing the home. Ultimately, everyone is personally responsible for either accepting or rejecting Jesus. But as a parent, it is my responsibility to share Jesus with my children. Furthermore, as a family member, it is my responsibility to talk to my family—close and extended—about Jesus and to live a life that reflects His love. It is not easy, but it is necessary.

Keys to Chapter Eleven:
- The *Shema* prayer was the basic confession of faith for the Jewish people.
- The *Shema* prayer is made up of three unifying parts:
    1. Deuteronomy 6:4-9—the confessional prayer.
    2. Deuteronomy 11:13-21—blessings for obedience and consequences for disobedience.
    3. Numbers 15:37-42—the importance of traditions.
- Four principles for evangelism and the family:
    1. Have a stated goal for parenting.
    2. Build your individual relationship with God.
    3. Practice what you preach.
    4. Teach your children about God consistently.
- Three ways to consistently teach our children about God: (1) informal teaching, (2) formal teaching, (3) family traditions.
- Loving God with all our heart, soul, and strength, means we love Him emotionally, passionately, and rationally; we are to feel Him intimately, commit to Him eternally, and serve Him practically.
- The goal of Christian education is to get God's Word in the minds of children so it affects their actions.
- A Christian family is a picture of life in the kingdom of God and is an evangelism tool in and of itself, pointing others to faith in Jesus.
- A Family Portrait (functional roles of family members): wives submit; husbands love; children obey; parents discipline.

Questions for Discussion:
1. What are some reasons why people have a difficult time discussing spiritual things with family members?
2. What are the four principles for evangelism and the family discussed in this chapter? Which one do you think is the most important? Why? Which one do you think is the most difficult? Why?
3. What do you think is the purpose of parenting? What are some goals you have to achieve that purpose?
4. What are some things you can do on a regular basis to build your relationship with God?
5. What do you think it means to say, "Your faith will be caught before it is taught"? How important is this to evangelizing your family?
6. How important are family traditions in teaching your children about God? What are some of your family traditions?
7. How, and in what ways, does a Christian family reflect life in God's kingdom, and how can such a family be a tool for evangelism?
8. What advice would you give to a spouse who has an unbelieving spouse? How would you encourage him or her?

12

Evangelism and the Great Commission

Has God ever rebuked you?
I am not talking about a harsh, judgmental, condemning rebuke, but a loving, parental, much-needed reminder of your own failure. To the believers in the church in Laodicea, God said, "Those whom I love I rebuke and discipline" (Revelation 3:19). Because we place our faith and trust in Christ and become God's children, we are spared from His wrath. Because God loves us, He no longer punishes us, but He does point out our wrongs, convicts of our sins, and instructs us on how to live a more holy life. God's rebuke is full of mercy and grace.

Have you ever needed a grace-filled rebuke from God?

I have received plenty of such rebukes, but one stands out in my memory more than others, and it has to do with my failure to proclaim that in and through Jesus, God's kingdom becomes a present reality.

I love to scuba dive. I go as often as I can and when I can't go, I dream of going by reading articles and looking at pictures in a few of my favorite diving magazines. Several years ago, over the Memorial Day weekend, a couple of friends from church and I drove to the Florida Panhandle to get wet.

It was a beautiful morning with sunny skies and calm seas as we loaded our gear onto the dive boat that would take us a few miles offshore of the Gulf of Mexico. The first dive was over an old tugboat that was sunk in about eighty feet of water. The second dive was over some bridge rubble in about sixty feet of water.

It was as we were loading our gear that I first noticed Robert. He looked like he had just rolled out of bed after a long night out with friends. Robert was in his mid-forties, had long stringy hair, and a mustache. He was thin and loud.

Robert looked like he had lived a pretty rough life partying, drinking, and more than likely, doing drugs. The T-shirt he wore was a blown-up photograph of a lady scantly covered in see-through lingerie. He made me uncomfortable. I determined not to make eye contact with Robert, hoping he would stay on his side of the boat and I would stay on mine. Robert was making his first two dives in the ocean, completing his Open Water Certification.[1]

The first dive went as scheduled. The water was clear and warm, and the fish were plentiful. It was a great dive. Between dives, Robert spoke loudly enough for everyone to hear. His stories were off-color and peppered with profanity. As he talked, the other divers nervously laughed. The second dive was as good as the first. Everything seemed to be normal until I reached the ladder at the back of the boat.

As I was about to climb the ladder, I noticed Robert lying on his back on the deck. Robert's color had already left him. The deckhand was frantically performing CPR. From my perspective, it already looked as if Robert was dead.

Once up the ladder, I quickly took my gear off and offered to help perform CPR. I told the deckhand we could take turns giving mouth-to-mouth and performing chest compressions. I began giving mouth-to-mouth and immediately noticed Robert was already cold. The captain had already notified the Coast Guard, but it would take a while to get all the divers on board. Once everyone was accounted for, the captain raced the engines and we took off for shore, knowing the Coast Guard was on their way out to meet us.

While traveling full speed, the Coast Guard's boat pulled up alongside us. With help from other divers, the paramedics jumped from their boat to ours. Completely exhausted, I stopped performing CPR and sat down. I knew Robert wasn't going to make it and I could tell by the expressions on the paramedics' faces that they knew it as well, but they kept performing their duties admirably.

As I sat there looking at Robert, experiencing this surreal scene, God lovingly rebuked me. God said, "Look at him. You prejudged, condemned, and completely ignored that man, and now he is in eternity."

In my spirit I tried to rationalize my lack of concern by replying, "Yea, but God, what was I supposed to do? There is nothing I could have said to Robert that would have changed how he had decided to live his life. I mean, come on, what are the odds that a chance encounter on a dive boat would have really altered his eternal outcome?"

Once again, God lovingly rebuked me, saying, "Kevin, you are missing the point. You are not responsible for the outcome. All I have asked you to do is show the love of Christ and live your life in such a way that, through your words and ac-

---

1. Open Water Certification is the first level of certification for recreational scuba diving.

tions, you demonstrate the reality of My kingdom. You didn't do that. In fact, you intentionally decided not to do that because Robert made you uncomfortable."

And then the Spirit brought these words of Jesus to my mind: "It is not the healthy who need a doctor, but the sick.... For I have not come to call the righteous, but sinners" (Matthew 9:12-13). I realized I was like the Pharisee who prayed, "God, I thank you that I am not like other men—robbers, evildoers, adulterers—or even like this tax collector" (Luke 18:11); or in my case, "like this scuba diver."

I had no choice but to repent and ask for—and receive—His forgiveness.

The Great Commission

Who is the Robert in your life? Who is the family member, or co-worker, or neighbor who makes you uncomfortable? Where was your chance encounter when, instead of engaging a person in a conversation, you ignored that person? What are we supposed to do?

Some of Jesus' last words to His disciples were, "All authority in heaven and on earth has been given to me. Therefore go and make disciples of all nations, baptizing them in the name of the Father and of the Son and of the Holy Spirit, and teaching them to obey everything I have commanded you. And surely I am with you always, to the very end of the age" (Matthew 28:18-20).

Immediately following Jesus' resurrection, the Jewish leaders devised a plan to proliferate the rumor that Jesus' disciples had stolen the body in the middle of the night. Roman soldiers were paid a large sum of money to help spread the rumor and falsify reports (see vv. 11-15). While these rumors spread, Jesus' disciples "went to Galilee, to the mountain where Jesus had told them to go" (v. 16). While we are not told which mountain, a hint of this prearranged meeting is seen in Jesus' words to His disciples on the night He was betrayed. Jesus said to them, "But after I have risen, I will go ahead of you into Galilee" (26:32). Then, on the morning of the resurrection, the angel said to the women who had gone to the tomb to anoint Jesus' body, "Go quickly and tell his disciples: 'He has risen from the dead and is going ahead of you into Galilee. There you will see him'" (28:7). As the women hurried away, they ran into Jesus who repeated the words of the angel: "Go and tell my brothers to go to Galilee; there they will see me" (v. 10). While the religious establishment was getting their "stories straight" so they could deny the resurrection of Jesus, the disciples were excitedly going to a prearranged location to meet the resurrected Jesus.

As soon as the disciples saw Jesus, "they worshiped him; but some doubted" (v. 17). In context, "doubted" does not signify disbelief but hesitation. The implication is some of the disciples immediately saw Jesus and worshiped Him, while others hesitated, not believing their eyes, but after a brief moment of uncertainty, worshiped Jesus along with the others.

It is in this context that Jesus instructed His disciples to go into the world and share the Gospel.

Like the first disciples, we live in a world where people are trying to discredit the resurrection of Christ and spread rumors about what actually happened on that first Easter morning. Our world is full of cynics, hypocrites, and sinners. Our world is full of people, like Robert, who make us uncomfortable. We would rather not interact with them—they can stay on their side of the world (the boat) and we can stay on our side. But these are the people to whom Jesus asked us to go and disciple, baptize, and teach. That is our challenge and our responsibility in the 21st century.

A key word, occurring four times in Matthew 28:18-20, is the word "all." The Greek word is *pas* and is translated "all" in verse 18, "all" in verse 19, and in verse 20 it is translated "everything" and then "always." Jesus is saying, "All authority . . . all nations . . . all things . . . all the days." The emphasis on "all" brings the entire biblical story to its ultimate climax. The resurrection did not give Jesus His authority; He had authority since before the beginning of time. God has always been interested in reaching every nation. God promised Abraham that through his descendants all the world would be blessed.[2] Peter wrote, "The Lord is not slow in keeping his promise, as some understand slowness. He is patient with you, not wanting anyone to perish, but everyone to come to repentance" (2 Peter 3:9). God's desire for His people has never been partial obedience, but full and complete obedience. James said, "Do not merely listen to the word, and so deceive yourselves. Do what it says" (James 1:22).[3] As we live a life of discipleship and obedience, sharing our faith, God has promised to never leave or forsake us. He will be with us until the end of time and eternity.

The command, or the commission, in these verses is not to "go," but to "make disciples." The Greek word translated "disciples" is *matheteuo*, and simply means "follower." The idea is a disciple is a student who is learning and being trained to take over the role of the teacher. The word "disciple," then, is analogous to "apprentice." A follower of Jesus is being taught, trained, and equipped to continue the ministry of Jesus. What was (and is) the ministry of Jesus? Proclaiming that in Him and through Him, God's kingdom becomes a present reality. In other words, Jesus' ministry and our ministry is to evangelize. Doing so is not an option but a command!

Baptism is the outward sign of an inward reality. Baptism identifies us with

---

2. See Genesis 12:3; 22:18; 26:4; 28:14; and Acts 3:25.

3. See also Matthew 7:21 and John 14:15. An entire list of biblical passages that discuss our complete obedience to God is too long to list.

the death, burial, and resurrection of Jesus Christ. The Greek word translated "teaching" is *didasko,* and means "to instruct" and "to learn." Followers of Jesus are always learning. It is important to note that baptism and teaching do not **make** a disciple (faith in Christ is what does that); rather, baptism and teaching are what it means **to be** a disciple. They are the consequence of discipleship, not the cause of discipleship.

Some Final Points

What is evangelism?

Evangelism is proclaiming the good news that the kingdom of God enters our reality in and through Jesus Christ. Evangelism in the 21st century is a whole lot like evangelism in the first century, and that excites me! If we, the body of Christ, will take evangelism seriously, we can turn our world upside down, just like the first disciples did. Jesus put it this way: "I tell you the truth, anyone who has faith in me will do what I have been doing. He will do even greater things than these, because I am going to the Father" (John 14:12).

There are five basic principles that, when applied, will help us stay focused on evangelism and the Great Commission:

1. *People are most effectively reached one at a time.*

Crusades, revival services, and special events are important, but God's plan for reaching all people is each disciple making disciples. There really is no "plan B." One person at a time was Jesus' model. He spoke to thousands and on a couple of occasions fed thousands, but His preferred method was to heal people one at a time and to call individuals, challenging them to forsake all and follow Him. Jesus continually pushed the crowds away, preferring to be alone with His close disciples. Jesus poured His life into a few people, who poured their lives into a few more people, who poured their lives into a few more people, and so on. In doing so, they changed the world.

Think of the people in your life who are far from God. Think of those within your circle of influence who need to hear about Jesus. There is no one more equipped to reach those you know than you. Make a list of people you know and begin praying for God to give you the opportunity to share the greatest news in the world. Jesus can change their present and transform their forever. Pray for God to give you the same boldness He gave the Apostle Paul, who said, "I am not ashamed of the gospel, because it is power of God for the salvation of everyone who believes" (Romans 1:16).

2. *Every person you meet needs to hear the Gospel.*

God does not bring people into your life by accident. Everyone—from your grumpy boss, to the cashier at the local grocery store, or a stranger on a dive boat—needs to hear the Gospel. This is the conviction you need in order to be motivated to share your faith. Without Jesus, people are lost and without hope. You have the good news they need to hear and want to hear. The Bible says, "For all have sinned and fall short of the glory of God" (Romans 3:23). Once again, the Apostle Paul wrote, "'Everyone who calls on the name of the Lord will be saved.' How, then, can they call on the one they have not believed in? And how can they believe in the one of whom they have not heard? And how can they hear without someone preaching to them? And how can they preach unless they are sent?" (10:13-15).

Your friends, family, and co-workers need to hear the good news. Right now, as in the days of the prophet Isaiah, God is asking, "Whom shall I send? And who will go for us?" (Isaiah 6:8). Will you respond like Isaiah and say, "Here am I. Send me!"

3. *Every person you meet has a need.*

There is an old saying that goes, "People don't care how much you know until they know how much you care."[4] People all around you are hurting. People all around you are longing for hope. It is no accident that Jesus met people's physical and emotional needs before He met their spiritual need of forgiveness from sins. Because of sin, people are broken and lost. Jesus, the Great Physician, wants to find us, heal us, and put us back together, making us whole. This is the meaning of salvation.

One of the best ways you can evangelize is by first meeting people's needs. It could be something as simple as cutting your neighbor's grass while they are out of town, to staying up with them and praying for them as they sit in the waiting room while their loved one is in critical surgery. It could be helping them with a water bill or a car repair, or driving them to and from dialysis. Everyone has a need and there are multiple ways you can meet those needs—big and small. Meeting those needs could very well open the door to a conversation about Jesus and God's kingdom. However—and this is extremely important—you continue to meet needs even if the person who has the need never accepts Jesus. Jesus said, "And if anyone gives even a cup of cold water to one of these little ones because he is my disciple, I tell you the truth, he will certainly not lose his reward" (Matthew 10:42).

4. *Every person eventually thinks about God.*

There is an avenue into every person's heart because every person eventually thinks about God. You can talk to anyone about God because eventually everyone asks himself or herself the question, "Is there a God, and if there is, how do I

---
4. From author's notes.

know Him and what does He expect of me?" The universal question, "Is there a God?" is one of the most compelling proofs of God's existence. In other words, if there is no God, then why the question?

This fact alone should give us confidence in sharing our faith. There is a common starting point. People have thought about the questions to which you have the answer. Sharing the good news of the reality of God's kingdom in Jesus Christ is the solution to the questions people ask.

5. *Every disciple of Jesus is expected to actively share his or her faith.*

One of the reasons God doesn't immediately transport us to heaven after conversion is because He wants us to share our story and His grace with other people. While some people have the spiritual gift of evangelism, all of us are called to evangelize. Jesus said we **will** be His witnesses (Acts 1:8). How we live our lives is a testimony of the Gospel. We are to look for opportunities to share our faith and we are to be ready at all times to share the reason for the hope we have. Sharing our faith is not an option—it is our highest obligation and our greatest privilege and responsibility.

Conclusion

I will never forget Robert and the loving rebuke God gave me that day. I pray I will never forget, and I pray I will never be the same.

The following day, after Robert's death, I called a friend who pastored a church in Atlanta, Georgia. I told him what happened and what God said. He listened and prayed for me. The next day, he called me back to tell me that Robert was from Atlanta and his tragic death made the newspaper. He took it upon himself to call Robert's mom and dad and tell them he knew a guy who was on the boat with Robert and who actually tried to save his life. He told them I was a minister and asked if it would be okay for him to give me their names and phone number, and if they would like me to call them. They said they would love to talk to me. I called and had a wonderful, heartfelt conversation with Robert's dad. He told me that Robert lived a rough life, but he had recently started to get his life together. Robert's dad told me the doctors had informed his wife and him that Robert died of a heart attack. I asked Robert's dad about God, Jesus, and church, and he said Robert believed in God, but he did not know anything beyond that. As a family, he told me, they only attended church sporadically. Robert's dad and I prayed together on the phone and to this day, I still pray for Robert's family and hope that somewhere in the midst of all his pain, Robert experienced the love, grace, and forgiveness of God. I am extremely thankful that though I failed to share my faith with Robert, I was given the opportunity to share my faith with his family. God is like that. He forgives us again and again and continues to give us opportunities to proclaim His kingdom to others.

I pray we will take advantage of every opportunity God gives us to evangelize in the 21st century.

Keys to Chapter Twelve:
- God's rebuke is full of mercy and grace.
- Our challenge in the 21st century is to go and disciple, baptize, and teach—even if going makes us uncomfortable.
- The command in the Great Commission is not to "go" but to "make disciples."
- A follower of Jesus is being taught, trained, and equipped to continue the ministry of Jesus.
- Jesus' ministry was proclaiming that in Him and through Him God's kingdom becomes a present reality. Jesus' ministry—and our ministry—is to evangelize. Doing so is not an option but a command.
- Baptizing and teaching do not make a disciple. Baptizing and teaching are what it means to be a disciple. Baptizing and teaching are the consequence of discipleship not the cause of discipleship.
- If the body of Christ would take evangelism seriously, we would turn our world upside down.
- Five principles for evangelism and the Great Commission:
    1. People are most effectively reached one at a time.
    2. Every person you meet needs to hear the Gospel.
    3. Every person you meet has a need.
    4. Every person eventually thinks about God.
    5. Every disciple of Jesus is expected to actively share his or her faith.
- Sharing our faith is not an option. It is our highest obligation and greatest privilege and responsibility.

Questions for Discussion:
1. Describe and discuss a time in your life when God had to lovingly rebuke you. What happened? How did you respond?
2. How do you think Jesus' disciples felt as they made their way to a prearranged meeting place to see the resurrected Jesus? What do you think was going through their minds? If you were one of the disciples, what question would you want to ask Jesus the moment you saw Him?

3. Would you have been one of the disciples who immediately worshiped Jesus or would you have been one of the disciples who hesitated? Discuss and explain your answer.

4. What do you think it means to be a disciple of Jesus? What do you think it means to say a follower of Jesus is being taught, trained, and equipped to continue Jesus' ministry?

5. How does understanding that Jesus' command in the Great Commission is not to "go" but to "make disciples"? Does it change your understanding at all? Why or why not?

6. This chapter explained five principles to help us stay focused on evangelism and the Great Commission. Which principle stood out the most to you? Why?

Made in United States
Orlando, FL
03 April 2022